C-4358   CAREER EXAMINATION SERIES

This is your
PASSBOOK for...

Traffic Clerk

Test Preparation Study Guide
Questions & Answers

NATIONAL LEARNING CORPORATION®

COPYRIGHT NOTICE

This book is SOLELY intended for, is sold ONLY to, and its use is RESTRICTED to individual, bona fide applicants or candidates who qualify by virtue of having seriously filed applications for appropriate license, certificate, professional and/or promotional advancement, higher school matriculation, scholarship, or other legitimate requirements of education and/or governmental authorities.

This book is NOT intended for use, class instruction, tutoring, training, duplication, copying, reprinting, excerption, or adaptation, etc., by:

1) Other publishers
2) Proprietors and/or Instructors of "Coaching" and/or Preparatory Courses
3) Personnel and/or Training Divisions of commercial, industrial, and governmental organizations
4) Schools, colleges, or universities and/or their departments and staffs, including teachers and other personnel
5) Testing Agencies or Bureaus
6) Study groups which seek by the purchase of a single volume to copy and/or duplicate and/or adapt this material for use by the group as a whole without having purchased individual volumes for each of the members of the group
7) Et al.

Such persons would be in violation of appropriate Federal and State statutes.

PROVISION OF LICENSING AGREEMENTS – Recognized educational, commercial, industrial, and governmental institutions and organizations, and others legitimately engaged in educational pursuits, including training, testing, and measurement activities, may address request for a licensing agreement to the copyright owners, who will determine whether, and under what conditions, including fees and charges, the materials in this book may be used them. In other words, a licensing facility exists for the legitimate use of the material in this book on other than an individual basis. However, it is asseverated and affirmed here that the material in this book CANNOT be used without the receipt of the express permission of such a licensing agreement from the Publishers. Inquiries re licensing should be addressed to the company, attention rights and permissions department.

All rights reserved, including the right of reproduction in whole or in part, in any form or by any means, electronic or mechanical, including photocopying, recording, or by any information storage and retrieval system, without permission in writing from the Publisher.

Copyright © 2025 by
National Learning Corporation

212 Michael Drive, Syosset, NY 11791
(516) 921-8888 • www.passbooks.com
E-mail: info@passbooks.com

PASSBOOK® SERIES

THE *PASSBOOK® SERIES* has been created to prepare applicants and candidates for the ultimate academic battlefield – the examination room.

At some time in our lives, each and every one of us may be required to take an examination – for validation, matriculation, admission, qualification, registration, certification, or licensure.

Based on the assumption that every applicant or candidate has met the basic formal educational standards, has taken the required number of courses, and read the necessary texts, the *PASSBOOK® SERIES* furnishes the one special preparation which may assure passing with confidence, instead of failing with insecurity. Examination questions – together with answers – are furnished as the basic vehicle for study so that the mysteries of the examination and its compounding difficulties may be eliminated or diminished by a sure method.

This book is meant to help you pass your examination provided that you qualify and are serious in your objective.

The entire field is reviewed through the huge store of content information which is succinctly presented through a provocative and challenging approach – the question-and-answer method.

A climate of success is established by furnishing the correct answers at the end of each test.

You soon learn to recognize types of questions, forms of questions, and patterns of questioning. You may even begin to anticipate expected outcomes.

You perceive that many questions are repeated or adapted so that you can gain acute insights, which may enable you to score many sure points.

You learn how to confront new questions, or types of questions, and to attack them confidently and work out the correct answers.

You note objectives and emphases, and recognize pitfalls and dangers, so that you may make positive educational adjustments.

Moreover, you are kept fully informed in relation to new concepts, methods, practices, and directions in the field.

You discover that you are actually taking the examination all the time: you are preparing for the examination by "taking" an examination, not by reading extraneous and/or supererogatory textbooks.

In short, this PASSBOOK®, used directedly, should be an important factor in helping you to pass your test.

TRAFFIC CLERK

DUTIES

Supervises staff, assigns and reviews work, including performance for compliance with instruction, procedures and standards for accuracy and completeness; assists in the preparation of procedures manual and devises work improvement methods; conducts on-the-job training and instructs staff in the implementation of work procedures to insure efficiency and effectiveness of operations; corresponds with the public and other city agencies concerning outstanding parking summonses, PVB procedures, towed vehicles, auction; etc.; oversees timely and accurate responses to all relevant and reasonable inquiries made by the public charged with parking violations; replies to written correspondence and telephone inquiries by providing required information and data; prepares and maintains complete and accurate records arid reports concerning towed vehicles, auctions and junk transfers, costs incurred by the City and payments received from vehicle releases and auto auctions; compiles information from periodic reports relative to parking violations, results of hearings and monetary payments; identifies production, operational and/or organizations problems and reports on same; records and responds to radio calls for towed vehicle requests and dispatches city-owned and private tow trucks; coordinates scheduling of individual cases for hearings and records disposition of the case; assists other sections of the bureau as needed; performs related duties as required.

SUBJECT OF EXAMINATION

The written test is designed to test for knowledge, skills, and/or abilities in such areas as:
1. Office management;
2. Supervision;
3. Clerical operations with letters and numbers;
4. Office record keeping;
5. Preparing written material; and
6. Understanding and interpreting written material.

HOW TO TAKE A TEST

I. YOU MUST PASS AN EXAMINATION

A. WHAT EVERY CANDIDATE SHOULD KNOW

Examination applicants often ask us for help in preparing for the written test. What can I study in advance? What kinds of questions will be asked? How will the test be given? How will the papers be graded?

As an applicant for a civil service examination, you may be wondering about some of these things. Our purpose here is to suggest effective methods of advance study and to describe civil service examinations.

Your chances for success on this examination can be increased if you know how to prepare. Those "pre-examination jitters" can be reduced if you know what to expect. You can even experience an adventure in good citizenship if you know why civil service exams are given.

B. WHY ARE CIVIL SERVICE EXAMINATIONS GIVEN?

Civil service examinations are important to you in two ways. As a citizen, you want public jobs filled by employees who know how to do their work. As a job seeker, you want a fair chance to compete for that job on an equal footing with other candidates. The best-known means of accomplishing this two-fold goal is the competitive examination.

Exams are widely publicized throughout the nation. They may be administered for jobs in federal, state, city, municipal, town or village governments or agencies.

Any citizen may apply, with some limitations, such as the age or residence of applicants. Your experience and education may be reviewed to see whether you meet the requirements for the particular examination. When these requirements exist, they are reasonable and applied consistently to all applicants. Thus, a competitive examination may cause you some uneasiness now, but it is your privilege and safeguard.

C. HOW ARE CIVIL SERVICE EXAMS DEVELOPED?

Examinations are carefully written by trained technicians who are specialists in the field known as "psychological measurement," in consultation with recognized authorities in the field of work that the test will cover. These experts recommend the subject matter areas or skills to be tested; only those knowledges or skills important to your success on the job are included. The most reliable books and source materials available are used as references. Together, the experts and technicians judge the difficulty level of the questions.

Test technicians know how to phrase questions so that the problem is clearly stated. Their ethics do not permit "trick" or "catch" questions. Questions may have been tried out on sample groups, or subjected to statistical analysis, to determine their usefulness.

Written tests are often used in combination with performance tests, ratings of training and experience, and oral interviews. All of these measures combine to form the best-known means of finding the right person for the right job.

II. HOW TO PASS THE WRITTEN TEST

A. NATURE OF THE EXAMINATION

To prepare intelligently for civil service examinations, you should know how they differ from school examinations you have taken. In school you were assigned certain definite pages to read or subjects to cover. The examination questions were quite detailed and usually emphasized memory. Civil service exams, on the other hand, try to discover your present ability to perform the duties of a position, plus your potentiality to learn these duties. In other words, a civil service exam attempts to predict how successful you will be. Questions cover such a broad area that they cannot be as minute and detailed as school exam questions.

In the public service similar kinds of work, or positions, are grouped together in one "class." This process is known as *position-classification*. All the positions in a class are paid according to the salary range for that class. One class title covers all of these positions, and they are all tested by the same examination.

B. FOUR BASIC STEPS

1) Study the announcement

How, then, can you know what subjects to study? Our best answer is: "Learn as much as possible about the class of positions for which you've applied." The exam will test the knowledge, skills and abilities needed to do the work.

Your most valuable source of information about the position you want is the official exam announcement. This announcement lists the training and experience qualifications. Check these standards and apply only if you come reasonably close to meeting them.

The brief description of the position in the examination announcement offers some clues to the subjects which will be tested. Think about the job itself. Review the duties in your mind. Can you perform them, or are there some in which you are rusty? Fill in the blank spots in your preparation.

Many jurisdictions preview the written test in the exam announcement by including a section called "Knowledge and Abilities Required," "Scope of the Examination," or some similar heading. Here you will find out specifically what fields will be tested.

2) Review your own background

Once you learn in general what the position is all about, and what you need to know to do the work, ask yourself which subjects you already know fairly well and which need improvement. You may wonder whether to concentrate on improving your strong areas or on building some background in your fields of weakness. When the announcement has specified "some knowledge" or "considerable knowledge," or has used adjectives like "beginning principles of..." or "advanced ... methods," you can get a clue as to the number and difficulty of questions to be asked in any given field. More questions, and hence broader coverage, would be included for those subjects which are more important in the work. Now weigh your strengths and weaknesses against the job requirements and prepare accordingly.

3) Determine the level of the position

Another way to tell how intensively you should prepare is to understand the level of the job for which you are applying. Is it the entering level? In other words, is this the position in which beginners in a field of work are hired? Or is it an intermediate or advanced level? Sometimes this is indicated by such words as "Junior" or "Senior" in the class title. Other jurisdictions use Roman numerals to designate the level – Clerk I, Clerk II, for example. The word "Supervisor" sometimes appears in the title. If the level is not indicated by the title, check the description of duties. Will you be working under very close supervision, or will you have responsibility for independent decisions in this work?

4) Choose appropriate study materials

Now that you know the subjects to be examined and the relative amount of each subject to be covered, you can choose suitable study materials. For beginning level jobs, or even advanced ones, if you have a pronounced weakness in some aspect of your training, read a modern, standard textbook in that field. Be sure it is up to date and has general coverage. Such books are normally available at your library, and the librarian will be glad to help you locate one. For entry-level positions, questions of appropriate difficulty are chosen – neither highly advanced questions, nor those too simple. Such questions require careful thought but not advanced training.

If the position for which you are applying is technical or advanced, you will read more advanced, specialized material. If you are already familiar with the basic principles of your field, elementary textbooks would waste your time. Concentrate on advanced textbooks and technical periodicals. Think through the concepts and review difficult problems in your field.

These are all general sources. You can get more ideas on your own initiative, following these leads. For example, training manuals and publications of the government agency which employs workers in your field can be useful, particularly for technical and professional positions. A letter or visit to the government department involved may result in more specific study suggestions, and certainly will provide you with a more definite idea of the exact nature of the position you are seeking.

III. KINDS OF TESTS

Tests are used for purposes other than measuring knowledge and ability to perform specified duties. For some positions, it is equally important to test ability to make adjustments to new situations or to profit from training. In others, basic mental abilities not dependent on information are essential. Questions which test these things may not appear as pertinent to the duties of the position as those which test for knowledge and information. Yet they are often highly important parts of a fair examination. For very general questions, it is almost impossible to help you direct your study efforts. What we can do is to point out some of the more common of these general abilities needed in public service positions and describe some typical questions.

1) General information

Broad, general information has been found useful for predicting job success in some kinds of work. This is tested in a variety of ways, from vocabulary lists to questions about current events. Basic background in some field of work, such as sociology or economics, may be sampled in a group of questions. Often these are principles which have become familiar to most persons through exposure rather than through formal training. It is difficult to advise you how to study for these questions; being alert to the world around you is our best suggestion.

2) Verbal ability

An example of an ability needed in many positions is verbal or language ability. Verbal ability is, in brief, the ability to use and understand words. Vocabulary and grammar tests are typical measures of this ability. Reading comprehension or paragraph interpretation questions are common in many kinds of civil service tests. You are given a paragraph of written material and asked to find its central meaning.

3) Numerical ability

Number skills can be tested by the familiar arithmetic problem, by checking paired lists of numbers to see which are alike and which are different, or by interpreting charts and graphs. In the latter test, a graph may be printed in the test booklet which you are asked to use as the basis for answering questions.

4) Observation

A popular test for law-enforcement positions is the observation test. A picture is shown to you for several minutes, then taken away. Questions about the picture test your ability to observe both details and larger elements.

5) Following directions

In many positions in the public service, the employee must be able to carry out written instructions dependably and accurately. You may be given a chart with several columns, each column listing a variety of information. The questions require you to carry out directions involving the information given in the chart.

6) Skills and aptitudes

Performance tests effectively measure some manual skills and aptitudes. When the skill is one in which you are trained, such as typing or shorthand, you can practice. These tests are often very much like those given in business school or high school courses. For many of the other skills and aptitudes, however, no short-time preparation can be made. Skills and abilities natural to you or that you have developed throughout your lifetime are being tested.

Many of the general questions just described provide all the data needed to answer the questions and ask you to use your reasoning ability to find the answers. Your best preparation for these tests, as well as for tests of facts and ideas, is to be at your physical and mental best. You, no doubt, have your own methods of getting into an exam-taking mood and keeping "in shape." The next section lists some ideas on this subject.

IV. KINDS OF QUESTIONS

Only rarely is the "essay" question, which you answer in narrative form, used in civil service tests. Civil service tests are usually of the short-answer type. Full instructions for answering these questions will be given to you at the examination. But in case this is your first experience with short-answer questions and separate answer sheets, here is what you need to know:

1) Multiple-choice Questions

Most popular of the short-answer questions is the "multiple choice" or "best answer" question. It can be used, for example, to test for factual knowledge, ability to solve problems or judgment in meeting situations found at work.

A multiple-choice question is normally one of three types—
- It can begin with an incomplete statement followed by several possible endings. You are to find the one ending which *best* completes the statement, although some of the others may not be entirely wrong.
- It can also be a complete statement in the form of a question which is answered by choosing one of the statements listed.

- It can be in the form of a problem – again you select the best answer.

Here is an example of a multiple-choice question with a discussion which should give you some clues as to the method for choosing the right answer:

When an employee has a complaint about his assignment, the action which will *best* help him overcome his difficulty is to
  A. discuss his difficulty with his coworkers
  B. take the problem to the head of the organization
  C. take the problem to the person who gave him the assignment
  D. say nothing to anyone about his complaint

In answering this question, you should study each of the choices to find which is best. Consider choice "A" – Certainly an employee may discuss his complaint with fellow employees, but no change or improvement can result, and the complaint remains unresolved. Choice "B" is a poor choice since the head of the organization probably does not know what assignment you have been given, and taking your problem to him is known as "going over the head" of the supervisor. The supervisor, or person who made the assignment, is the person who can clarify it or correct any injustice. Choice "C" is, therefore, correct. To say nothing, as in choice "D," is unwise. Supervisors have and interest in knowing the problems employees are facing, and the employee is seeking a solution to his problem.

2) True/False Questions

The "true/false" or "right/wrong" form of question is sometimes used. Here a complete statement is given. Your job is to decide whether the statement is right or wrong.

SAMPLE: A roaming cell-phone call to a nearby city costs less than a non-roaming call to a distant city.

This statement is wrong, or false, since roaming calls are more expensive.

This is not a complete list of all possible question forms, although most of the others are variations of these common types. You will always get complete directions for answering questions. Be sure you understand *how* to mark your answers – ask questions until you do.

V. RECORDING YOUR ANSWERS

Computer terminals are used more and more today for many different kinds of exams.

For an examination with very few applicants, you may be told to record your answers in the test booklet itself. Separate answer sheets are much more common. If this separate answer sheet is to be scored by machine – and this is often the case – it is highly important that you mark your answers correctly in order to get credit.

An electronic scoring machine is often used in civil service offices because of the speed with which papers can be scored. Machine-scored answer sheets must be marked with a pencil, which will be given to you. This pencil has a high graphite content which responds to the electronic scoring machine. As a matter of fact, stray dots may register as answers, so do not let your pencil rest on the answer sheet while you are pondering the correct answer. Also, if your pencil lead breaks or is otherwise defective, ask for another.

Since the answer sheet will be dropped in a slot in the scoring machine, be careful not to bend the corners or get the paper crumpled.

The answer sheet normally has five vertical columns of numbers, with 30 numbers to a column. These numbers correspond to the question numbers in your test booklet. After each number, going across the page are four or five pairs of dotted lines. These short dotted lines have small letters or numbers above them. The first two pairs may also have a "T" or "F" above the letters. This indicates that the first two pairs only are to be used if the questions are of the true-false type. If the questions are multiple choice, disregard the "T" and "F" and pay attention only to the small letters or numbers.

Answer your questions in the manner of the sample that follows:

32. The largest city in the United States is
    A. Washington, D.C.
    B. New York City
    C. Chicago
    D. Detroit
    E. San Francisco

1) Choose the answer you think is best. (New York City is the largest, so "B" is correct.)
2) Find the row of dotted lines numbered the same as the question you are answering. (Find row number 32)
3) Find the pair of dotted lines corresponding to the answer. (Find the pair of lines under the mark "B.")
4) Make a solid black mark between the dotted lines.

VI. BEFORE THE TEST

Common sense will help you find procedures to follow to get ready for an examination. Too many of us, however, overlook these sensible measures. Indeed, nervousness and fatigue have been found to be the most serious reasons why applicants fail to do their best on civil service tests. Here is a list of reminders:

- Begin your preparation early – Don't wait until the last minute to go scurrying around for books and materials or to find out what the position is all about.
- Prepare continuously – An hour a night for a week is better than an all-night cram session. This has been definitely established. What is more, a night a week for a month will return better dividends than crowding your study into a shorter period of time.
- Locate the place of the exam – You have been sent a notice telling you when and where to report for the examination. If the location is in a different town or otherwise unfamiliar to you, it would be well to inquire the best route and learn something about the building.
- Relax the night before the test – Allow your mind to rest. Do not study at all that night. Plan some mild recreation or diversion; then go to bed early and get a good night's sleep.
- Get up early enough to make a leisurely trip to the place for the test – This way unforeseen events, traffic snarls, unfamiliar buildings, etc. will not upset you.
- Dress comfortably – A written test is not a fashion show. You will be known by number and not by name, so wear something comfortable.

- Leave excess paraphernalia at home – Shopping bags and odd bundles will get in your way. You need bring only the items mentioned in the official notice you received; usually everything you need is provided. Do not bring reference books to the exam. They will only confuse those last minutes and be taken away from you when in the test room.
- Arrive somewhat ahead of time – If because of transportation schedules you must get there very early, bring a newspaper or magazine to take your mind off yourself while waiting.
- Locate the examination room – When you have found the proper room, you will be directed to the seat or part of the room where you will sit. Sometimes you are given a sheet of instructions to read while you are waiting. Do not fill out any forms until you are told to do so; just read them and be prepared.
- Relax and prepare to listen to the instructions
- If you have any physical problem that may keep you from doing your best, be sure to tell the test administrator. If you are sick or in poor health, you really cannot do your best on the exam. You can come back and take the test some other time.

VII. AT THE TEST

The day of the test is here and you have the test booklet in your hand. The temptation to get going is very strong. Caution! There is more to success than knowing the right answers. You must know how to identify your papers and understand variations in the type of short-answer question used in this particular examination. Follow these suggestions for maximum results from your efforts:

1) Cooperate with the monitor

The test administrator has a duty to create a situation in which you can be as much at ease as possible. He will give instructions, tell you when to begin, check to see that you are marking your answer sheet correctly, and so on. He is not there to guard you, although he will see that your competitors do not take unfair advantage. He wants to help you do your best.

2) Listen to all instructions

Don't jump the gun! Wait until you understand all directions. In most civil service tests you get more time than you need to answer the questions. So don't be in a hurry. Read each word of instructions until you clearly understand the meaning. Study the examples, listen to all announcements and follow directions. Ask questions if you do not understand what to do.

3) Identify your papers

Civil service exams are usually identified by number only. You will be assigned a number; you must not put your name on your test papers. Be sure to copy your number correctly. Since more than one exam may be given, copy your exact examination title.

4) Plan your time

Unless you are told that a test is a "speed" or "rate of work" test, speed itself is usually not important. Time enough to answer all the questions will be provided, but this does not mean that you have all day. An overall time limit has been set. Divide the total time (in minutes) by the number of questions to determine the approximate time you have for each question.

5) Do not linger over difficult questions

If you come across a difficult question, mark it with a paper clip (useful to have along) and come back to it when you have been through the booklet. One caution if you do this – be sure to skip a number on your answer sheet as well. Check often to be sure that you have not lost your place and that you are marking in the row numbered the same as the question you are answering.

6) Read the questions

Be sure you know what the question asks! Many capable people are unsuccessful because they failed to *read* the questions correctly.

7) Answer all questions

Unless you have been instructed that a penalty will be deducted for incorrect answers, it is better to guess than to omit a question.

8) Speed tests

It is often better NOT to guess on speed tests. It has been found that on timed tests people are tempted to spend the last few seconds before time is called in marking answers at random – without even reading them – in the hope of picking up a few extra points. To discourage this practice, the instructions may warn you that your score will be "corrected" for guessing. That is, a penalty will be applied. The incorrect answers will be deducted from the correct ones, or some other penalty formula will be used.

9) Review your answers

If you finish before time is called, go back to the questions you guessed or omitted to give them further thought. Review other answers if you have time.

10) Return your test materials

If you are ready to leave before others have finished or time is called, take ALL your materials to the monitor and leave quietly. Never take any test material with you. The monitor can discover whose papers are not complete, and taking a test booklet may be grounds for disqualification.

VIII. EXAMINATION TECHNIQUES

1) Read the general instructions carefully. These are usually printed on the first page of the exam booklet. As a rule, these instructions refer to the timing of the examination; the fact that you should not start work until the signal and must stop work at a signal, etc. If there are any *special* instructions, such as a choice of questions to be answered, make sure that you note this instruction carefully.

2) When you are ready to start work on the examination, that is as soon as the signal has been given, read the instructions to each question booklet, underline any key words or phrases, such as *least*, *best*, *outline*, *describe* and the like. In this way you will tend to answer as requested rather than discover on reviewing your paper that you *listed without describing*, that you selected the *worst* choice rather than the *best* choice, etc.

3) If the examination is of the objective or multiple-choice type – that is, each question will also give a series of possible answers: A, B, C or D, and you are called upon to select the best answer and write the letter next to that answer on your answer paper – it is advisable to start answering each question in turn. There may be anywhere from 50 to 100 such questions in the three or four hours allotted and you can see how much time would be taken if you read through all the questions before beginning to answer any. Furthermore, if you come across a question or group of questions which you know would be difficult to answer, it would undoubtedly affect your handling of all the other questions.

4) If the examination is of the essay type and contains but a few questions, it is a moot point as to whether you should read all the questions before starting to answer any one. Of course, if you are given a choice – say five out of seven and the like – then it is essential to read all the questions so you can eliminate the two that are most difficult. If, however, you are asked to answer all the questions, there may be danger in trying to answer the easiest one first because you may find that you will spend too much time on it. The best technique is to answer the first question, then proceed to the second, etc.

5) Time your answers. Before the exam begins, write down the time it started, then add the time allowed for the examination and write down the time it must be completed, then divide the time available somewhat as follows:
   - If 3-1/2 hours are allowed, that would be 210 minutes. If you have 80 objective-type questions, that would be an average of 2-1/2 minutes per question. Allow yourself no more than 2 minutes per question, or a total of 160 minutes, which will permit about 50 minutes to review.
   - If for the time allotment of 210 minutes there are 7 essay questions to answer, that would average about 30 minutes a question. Give yourself only 25 minutes per question so that you have about 35 minutes to review.

6) The most important instruction is to *read each question* and make sure you know what is wanted. The second most important instruction is to *time yourself properly* so that you answer every question. The third most important instruction is to *answer every question*. Guess if you have to but include something for each question. Remember that you will receive no credit for a blank and will probably receive some credit if you write something in answer to an essay question. If you guess a letter – say "B" for a multiple-choice question – you may have guessed right. If you leave a blank as an answer to a multiple-choice question, the examiners may respect your feelings but it will not add a point to your score. Some exams may penalize you for wrong answers, so in such cases *only*, you may not want to guess unless you have some basis for your answer.

7) Suggestions
   a. Objective-type questions
      1. Examine the question booklet for proper sequence of pages and questions
      2. Read all instructions carefully
      3. Skip any question which seems too difficult; return to it after all other questions have been answered
      4. Apportion your time properly; do not spend too much time on any single question or group of questions

5. Note and underline key words – *all, most, fewest, least, best, worst, same, opposite,* etc.
6. Pay particular attention to negatives
7. Note unusual option, e.g., unduly long, short, complex, different or similar in content to the body of the question
8. Observe the use of "hedging" words – *probably, may, most likely,* etc.
9. Make sure that your answer is put next to the same number as the question
10. Do not second-guess unless you have good reason to believe the second answer is definitely more correct
11. Cross out original answer if you decide another answer is more accurate; do not erase until you are ready to hand your paper in
12. Answer all questions; guess unless instructed otherwise
13. Leave time for review

b. Essay questions
1. Read each question carefully
2. Determine exactly what is wanted. Underline key words or phrases.
3. Decide on outline or paragraph answer
4. Include many different points and elements unless asked to develop any one or two points or elements
5. Show impartiality by giving pros and cons unless directed to select one side only
6. Make and write down any assumptions you find necessary to answer the questions
7. Watch your English, grammar, punctuation and choice of words
8. Time your answers; don't crowd material

8) Answering the essay question

Most essay questions can be answered by framing the specific response around several key words or ideas. Here are a few such key words or ideas:

M's: manpower, materials, methods, money, management
P's: purpose, program, policy, plan, procedure, practice, problems, pitfalls, personnel, public relations

  a. Six basic steps in handling problems:
1. Preliminary plan and background development
2. Collect information, data and facts
3. Analyze and interpret information, data and facts
4. Analyze and develop solutions as well as make recommendations
5. Prepare report and sell recommendations
6. Install recommendations and follow up effectiveness

  b. Pitfalls to avoid
1. *Taking things for granted* – A statement of the situation does not necessarily imply that each of the elements is necessarily true; for example, a complaint may be invalid and biased so that all that can be taken for granted is that a complaint has been registered

2. *Considering only one side of a situation* – Wherever possible, indicate several alternatives and then point out the reasons you selected the best one
3. *Failing to indicate follow up* – Whenever your answer indicates action on your part, make certain that you will take proper follow-up action to see how successful your recommendations, procedures or actions turn out to be
4. *Taking too long in answering any single question* – Remember to time your answers properly

IX. AFTER THE TEST

Scoring procedures differ in detail among civil service jurisdictions although the general principles are the same. Whether the papers are hand-scored or graded by machine we have described, they are nearly always graded by number. That is, the person who marks the paper knows only the number – never the name – of the applicant. Not until all the papers have been graded will they be matched with names. If other tests, such as training and experience or oral interview ratings have been given, scores will be combined. Different parts of the examination usually have different weights. For example, the written test might count 60 percent of the final grade, and a rating of training and experience 40 percent. In many jurisdictions, veterans will have a certain number of points added to their grades.

After the final grade has been determined, the names are placed in grade order and an eligible list is established. There are various methods for resolving ties between those who get the same final grade – probably the most common is to place first the name of the person whose application was received first. Job offers are made from the eligible list in the order the names appear on it. You will be notified of your grade and your rank as soon as all these computations have been made. This will be done as rapidly as possible.

People who are found to meet the requirements in the announcement are called "eligibles." Their names are put on a list of eligible candidates. An eligible's chances of getting a job depend on how high he stands on this list and how fast agencies are filling jobs from the list.

When a job is to be filled from a list of eligibles, the agency asks for the names of people on the list of eligibles for that job. When the civil service commission receives this request, it sends to the agency the names of the three people highest on this list. Or, if the job to be filled has specialized requirements, the office sends the agency the names of the top three persons who meet these requirements from the general list.

The appointing officer makes a choice from among the three people whose names were sent to him. If the selected person accepts the appointment, the names of the others are put back on the list to be considered for future openings.

That is the rule in hiring from all kinds of eligible lists, whether they are for typist, carpenter, chemist, or something else. For every vacancy, the appointing officer has his choice of any one of the top three eligibles on the list. This explains why the person whose name is on top of the list sometimes does not get an appointment when some of the persons lower on the list do. If the appointing officer chooses the second or third eligible, the No. 1 eligible does not get a job at once, but stays on the list until he is appointed or the list is terminated.

X. HOW TO PASS THE INTERVIEW TEST

The examination for which you applied requires an oral interview test. You have already taken the written test and you are now being called for the interview test – the final part of the formal examination.

You may think that it is not possible to prepare for an interview test and that there are no procedures to follow during an interview. Our purpose is to point out some things you can do in advance that will help you and some good rules to follow and pitfalls to avoid while you are being interviewed.

What is an interview supposed to test?

The written examination is designed to test the technical knowledge and competence of the candidate; the oral is designed to evaluate intangible qualities, not readily measured otherwise, and to establish a list showing the relative fitness of each candidate – as measured against his competitors – for the position sought. Scoring is not on the basis of "right" and "wrong," but on a sliding scale of values ranging from "not passable" to "outstanding." As a matter of fact, it is possible to achieve a relatively low score without a single "incorrect" answer because of evident weakness in the qualities being measured.

Occasionally, an examination may consist entirely of an oral test – either an individual or a group oral. In such cases, information is sought concerning the technical knowledges and abilities of the candidate, since there has been no written examination for this purpose. More commonly, however, an oral test is used to supplement a written examination.

Who conducts interviews?

The composition of oral boards varies among different jurisdictions. In nearly all, a representative of the personnel department serves as chairman. One of the members of the board may be a representative of the department in which the candidate would work. In some cases, "outside experts" are used, and, frequently, a businessman or some other representative of the general public is asked to serve. Labor and management or other special groups may be represented. The aim is to secure the services of experts in the appropriate field.

However the board is composed, it is a good idea (and not at all improper or unethical) to ascertain in advance of the interview who the members are and what groups they represent. When you are introduced to them, you will have some idea of their backgrounds and interests, and at least you will not stutter and stammer over their names.

What should be done before the interview?

While knowledge about the board members is useful and takes some of the surprise element out of the interview, there is other preparation which is more substantive. It *is* possible to prepare for an oral interview – in several ways:

1) Keep a copy of your application and review it carefully before the interview

This may be the only document before the oral board, and the starting point of the interview. Know what education and experience you have listed there, and the sequence and dates of all of it. Sometimes the board will ask you to review the highlights of your experience for them; you should not have to hem and haw doing it.

2) Study the class specification and the examination announcement

Usually, the oral board has one or both of these to guide them. The qualities, characteristics or knowledges required by the position sought are stated in these documents. They offer valuable clues as to the nature of the oral interview. For example, if the job involves supervisory responsibilities, the announcement will usually indicate that knowledge of modern supervisory methods and the qualifications of the candidate as a supervisor will be tested. If so, you can expect such questions, frequently in the form of a hypothetical situation which you are expected to solve. NEVER go into an oral without knowledge of the duties and responsibilities of the job you seek.

3) Think through each qualification required

Try to visualize the kind of questions you would ask if you were a board member. How well could you answer them? Try especially to appraise your own knowledge and background in each area, *measured against the job sought*, and identify any areas in which you are weak. Be critical and realistic – do not flatter yourself.

4) Do some general reading in areas in which you feel you may be weak

For example, if the job involves supervision and your past experience has NOT, some general reading in supervisory methods and practices, particularly in the field of human relations, might be useful. Do NOT study agency procedures or detailed manuals. The oral board will be testing your understanding and capacity, not your memory.

5) Get a good night's sleep and watch your general health and mental attitude

You will want a clear head at the interview. Take care of a cold or any other minor ailment, and of course, no hangovers.

What should be done on the day of the interview?

Now comes the day of the interview itself. Give yourself plenty of time to get there. Plan to arrive somewhat ahead of the scheduled time, particularly if your appointment is in the fore part of the day. If a previous candidate fails to appear, the board might be ready for you a bit early. By early afternoon an oral board is almost invariably behind schedule if there are many candidates, and you may have to wait. Take along a book or magazine to read, or your application to review, but leave any extraneous material in the waiting room when you go in for your interview. In any event, relax and compose yourself.

The matter of dress is important. The board is forming impressions about you – from your experience, your manners, your attitude, and your appearance. Give your personal appearance careful attention. Dress your best, but not your flashiest. Choose conservative, appropriate clothing, and be sure it is immaculate. This is a business interview, and your appearance should indicate that you regard it as such. Besides, being well groomed and properly dressed will help boost your confidence.

Sooner or later, someone will call your name and escort you into the interview room. *This is it*. From here on you are on your own. It is too late for any more preparation. But remember, you asked for this opportunity to prove your fitness, and you are here because your request was granted.

What happens when you go in?

The usual sequence of events will be as follows: The clerk (who is often the board stenographer) will introduce you to the chairman of the oral board, who will introduce you to the other members of the board. Acknowledge the introductions before you sit down. Do not be surprised if you find a microphone facing you or a stenotypist sitting by. Oral interviews are usually recorded in the event of an appeal or other review.

Usually the chairman of the board will open the interview by reviewing the highlights of your education and work experience from your application – primarily for the benefit of the other members of the board, as well as to get the material into the record. Do not interrupt or comment unless there is an error or significant misinterpretation; if that is the case, do not hesitate. But do not quibble about insignificant matters. Also, he will usually ask you some question about your education, experience or your present job – partly to get you to start talking and to establish the interviewing "rapport." He may start the actual questioning, or turn it over to one of the other members. Frequently, each member undertakes the questioning on a particular area, one in which he is perhaps most competent, so you can expect each member to participate in the examination. Because time is limited, you may also expect some rather abrupt switches in the direction the questioning takes, so do not be upset by it. Normally, a board member will not pursue a single line of questioning unless he discovers a particular strength or weakness.

After each member has participated, the chairman will usually ask whether any member has any further questions, then will ask you if you have anything you wish to add. Unless you are expecting this question, it may floor you. Worse, it may start you off on an extended, extemporaneous speech. The board is not usually seeking more information. The question is principally to offer you a last opportunity to present further qualifications or to indicate that you have nothing to add. So, if you feel that a significant qualification or characteristic has been overlooked, it is proper to point it out in a sentence or so. Do not compliment the board on the thoroughness of their examination – they have been sketchy, and you know it. If you wish, merely say, "No thank you, I have nothing further to add." This is a point where you can "talk yourself out" of a good impression or fail to present an important bit of information. Remember, *you close the interview yourself*.

The chairman will then say, "That is all, Mr. _____, thank you." Do not be startled; the interview is over, and quicker than you think. Thank him, gather your belongings and take your leave. Save your sigh of relief for the other side of the door.

How to put your best foot forward

Throughout this entire process, you may feel that the board individually and collectively is trying to pierce your defenses, seek out your hidden weaknesses and embarrass and confuse you. Actually, this is not true. They are obliged to make an appraisal of your qualifications for the job you are seeking, and they want to see you in your best light. Remember, they must interview all candidates and a non-cooperative candidate may become a failure in spite of their best efforts to bring out his qualifications. Here are 15 suggestions that will help you:

1) Be natural – Keep your attitude confident, not cocky

If you are not confident that you can do the job, do not expect the board to be. Do not apologize for your weaknesses, try to bring out your strong points. The board is interested in a positive, not negative, presentation. Cockiness will antagonize any board member and make him wonder if you are covering up a weakness by a false show of strength.

2) Get comfortable, but don't lounge or sprawl

Sit erectly but not stiffly. A careless posture may lead the board to conclude that you are careless in other things, or at least that you are not impressed by the importance of the occasion. Either conclusion is natural, even if incorrect. Do not fuss with your clothing, a pencil or an ashtray. Your hands may occasionally be useful to emphasize a point; do not let them become a point of distraction.

3) Do not wisecrack or make small talk

This is a serious situation, and your attitude should show that you consider it as such. Further, the time of the board is limited – they do not want to waste it, and neither should you.

4) Do not exaggerate your experience or abilities

In the first place, from information in the application or other interviews and sources, the board may know more about you than you think. Secondly, you probably will not get away with it. An experienced board is rather adept at spotting such a situation, so do not take the chance.

5) If you know a board member, do not make a point of it, yet do not hide it

Certainly you are not fooling him, and probably not the other members of the board. Do not try to take advantage of your acquaintanceship – it will probably do you little good.

6) Do not dominate the interview

Let the board do that. They will give you the clues – do not assume that you have to do all the talking. Realize that the board has a number of questions to ask you, and do not try to take up all the interview time by showing off your extensive knowledge of the answer to the first one.

7) Be attentive

You only have 20 minutes or so, and you should keep your attention at its sharpest throughout. When a member is addressing a problem or question to you, give him your undivided attention. Address your reply principally to him, but do not exclude the other board members.

8) Do not interrupt

A board member may be stating a problem for you to analyze. He will ask you a question when the time comes. Let him state the problem, and wait for the question.

9) Make sure you understand the question

Do not try to answer until you are sure what the question is. If it is not clear, restate it in your own words or ask the board member to clarify it for you. However, do not haggle about minor elements.

10) Reply promptly but not hastily

A common entry on oral board rating sheets is "candidate responded readily," or "candidate hesitated in replies." Respond as promptly and quickly as you can, but do not jump to a hasty, ill-considered answer.

11) Do not be peremptory in your answers

A brief answer is proper – but do not fire your answer back. That is a losing game from your point of view. The board member can probably ask questions much faster than you can answer them.

12) Do not try to create the answer you think the board member wants

He is interested in what kind of mind you have and how it works – not in playing games. Furthermore, he can usually spot this practice and will actually grade you down on it.

13) Do not switch sides in your reply merely to agree with a board member

Frequently, a member will take a contrary position merely to draw you out and to see if you are willing and able to defend your point of view. Do not start a debate, yet do not surrender a good position. If a position is worth taking, it is worth defending.

14) Do not be afraid to admit an error in judgment if you are shown to be wrong

The board knows that you are forced to reply without any opportunity for careful consideration. Your answer may be demonstrably wrong. If so, admit it and get on with the interview.

15) Do not dwell at length on your present job

The opening question may relate to your present assignment. Answer the question but do not go into an extended discussion. You are being examined for a *new* job, not your present one. As a matter of fact, try to phrase ALL your answers in terms of the job for which you are being examined.

Basis of Rating

Probably you will forget most of these "do's" and "don'ts" when you walk into the oral interview room. Even remembering them all will not ensure you a passing grade. Perhaps you did not have the qualifications in the first place. But remembering them will help you to put your best foot forward, without treading on the toes of the board members.

Rumor and popular opinion to the contrary notwithstanding, an oral board wants you to make the best appearance possible. They know you are under pressure – but they also want to see how you respond to it as a guide to what your reaction would be under the pressures of the job you seek. They will be influenced by the degree of poise you display, the personal traits you show and the manner in which you respond.

ABOUT THIS BOOK

This book contains tests divided into Examination Sections. Go through each test, answering every question in the margin. We have also attached a sample answer sheet at the back of the book that can be removed and used. At the end of each test look at the answer key and check your answers. On the ones you got wrong, look at the right answer choice and learn. Do not fill in the answers first. Do not memorize the questions and answers, but understand the answer and principles involved. On your test, the questions will likely be different from the samples. Questions are changed and new ones added. If you understand these past questions you should have success with any changes that arise. Tests may consist of several types of questions. We have additional books on each subject should more study be advisable or necessary for you. Finally, the more you study, the better prepared you will be. This book is intended to be the last thing you study before you walk into the examination room. Prior study of relevant texts is also recommended. NLC publishes some of these in our Fundamental Series. Knowledge and good sense are important factors in passing your exam. Good luck also helps. So now study this Passbook, absorb the material contained within and take that knowledge into the examination. Then do your best to pass that exam.

EXAMINATION SECTION

EXAMINATION SECTION
TEST 1

DIRECTIONS: Each question or incomplete statement is followed by several suggested answers or completions. Select the one that BEST answers the question or completes the statement. *PRINT THE LETTER OF THE CORRECT ANSWER IN THE SPACE AT THE RIGHT.*

1. A BASIC method of operation that a good supervisor should follow is to

    A. check the work of subordinates constantly to make sure they are not making exceptions to the rules
    B. train subordinates so they can handle problems that come up regularly themselves and come to him only with special cases
    C. delegate to subordinates only those duties which he cannot do himself
    D. issue directions to subordinates only on special matters

2. To do a good job of performance evaluation, it is BEST for a supervisor to

    A. compare the employees performance to that of another employee doing similar work
    B. give greatest weight to instances of unusually good or unusually poor performance
    C. leave out any consideration of the employees personal traits
    D. measure the employees performance against standard performance requirements

3. Of the following, the MOST important reason for a supervisor to have private face-to-face discussions with subordinates about their performance is to

    A. help employees improve their work
    B. give special praise to employees who perform well
    C. encourage the employees to compete for higher performance ratings
    D. discipline employees who perform poorly

4. Of the following, the CHIEF purpose of a probationary period for a new employee is to allow time for

    A. finding out whether the selection processes are satisfactory
    B. the employee to make adjustments in his home circumstances made necessary by the job
    C. the employee to decide whether he wants a permanent appointment
    D. determining the fitness of the employee to continue in the job

5. When an enforcement agent resigns his job, it is MOST important to conduct an *exit interview* in order to

    A. try to get the employee to remain on the job
    B. learn the true reasons for the employees resignation
    C. see that the employee leaves with a good opinion of the agency
    D. ask the agent if he would consider a transfer

6. Chronic lateness of employees is generally LEAST likely to be due to

    A. distance of job location from home
    B. poor personnel administration

C. unexpressed employee grievances
D. low morale

7. Of the following, the LEAST effective stimulus for motivating employees toward improved performance over a long-range period is

   A. their sense of achievement
   B. their feeling of recognition
   C. opportunity for their self-development
   D. an increase in salary

8. Suppose that not one of a group of employees has turned in an idea to the employees suggestion system during the past year.
   The MOST probable reason for this situation is that the

   A. money awards given for suggestions used are not high enough to make employees interested
   B. employees in this group are not able to develop any good ideas
   C. supervisor of these employees is not doing enough to encourage them to take part in the program
   D. methods and procedures of operation do not need improvement

9. A subordinate tells you that he is having trouble concentrating on his work due to a personal problem at home.
   Of the following, it would be BEST for you to

   A. refer him to a community service agency
   B. listen quietly to the story because he may just need a sympathetic ear
   C. tell him that you cannot help him because the problem is not job related
   D. ask him some questions about the nature of the problem and tell him how you would handle it

10. For you as a supervisor to give each of your subordinates EXACTLY the same type of supervision is

    A. *advisable,* because doing this insures fair and impartial treatment of each individual
    B. *not advisable,* because individuals like to think that they are receiving better treatment than others
    C. *advisable,* because once a supervisor learns how to deal with a subordinate who brings a problem to him, he can handle another subordinate with this problem in the same way
    D. *not advisable,* because each person is different, and there is no one supervisory procedure for dealing with individuals that applies in every case

11. A senior enforcement agent under your supervision tells you that he is reluctant to speak to one of the agents about his poor work habits, because this agent is *strong-willed* and he does not want to antagonize him.
    For you to offer to speak to the agent about this matter yourself would be

    A. *advisable,* since you are in a position of greater authority
    B. *inadvisable,* since handling this problem is a basic supervisory responsibility of the senior agent

C. *advisable,* since the senior agent must work more closely with the agent than you do
D. *inadvisable,* since you should not risk antagonizing the agent yourself

12. Some of your subordinates have been coming to you with complaints you feel are unimportant. For you to hear their stories out is

    A. *poor* practice; you should spend your time on more important matters
    B. *good* practice; this will increase your popularity with your subordinates
    C. *poor* practice; subordinates should learn to come to you only with major grievances
    D. *good* practice; it may prevent minor complaints from developing into major grievances

13. Assume that an agency has an established procedure for handling employee grievances. An employee in this agency comes to his immediate supervisor with a grievance. The supervisor investigates the matter and makes a decision. However, the employee is not satisfied with the decision made by the supervisor.
    The BEST action for the supervisor to take is to

    A. tell the employee he will review the matter further
    B. remind the employee that he is the supervisor and the employee must act in accordance with his decision
    C. explain to the employee how he can carry his complaint forward to the next step in the grievance procedure
    D. tell the employee he will consult with his own superiors on the matter

14. Enforcement agents and senior enforcement agents often must make quick decisions while in the field. The district commander can BEST help subordinates meet such situations by

    A. training them in the appropriate action to take for every problem that may come up
    B. limiting the areas in which they are permitted to make decisions
    C. making certain they understand clearly the basic policies of the bureau and the department
    D. delegating authority to make such decisions to only a few subordinates on each level

15. Studies have shown that the CHIEF cause of failure to achieve success as a supervisor is

    A. an unwillingness to delegate authority to subordinates
    B. the establishment of high performance standards for subordinates
    C. the use of discipline that is too strict
    D. showing too much leniency to poor workers

16. When a supervisor delegates to a subordinate certain work that he normally does himself, it is MOST important that he give the subordinate

    A. responsibility for also setting the standards for the work to be done
    B. sufficient authority to be able to carry out the assignment
    C. written, step-by-step instructions for doing the work
    D. an explanation of one part of the task at a time

17. It is particularly important that disciplinary actions be equitable as between individuals. This statement implies that

    A. punishment applied in disciplinary actions should be lenient
    B. proposed disciplinary actions should be reviewed by higher authority
    C. subordinates should have an opportunity to present their stories before penalties are applied
    D. penalties for violations of the rules should be standardized and consistently applied

18. You discover that from time to time a number of false rumors circulate among your subordinates.
    Of the following, the BEST way for you to handle this situation is to

    A. ignore the rumors since rumors circulate in every office and can never be eliminated
    B. attempt to find those responsible for the rumors and reprimand them
    C. make sure that your employees are informed as soon as possible about all matters that affect them
    D. inform your superior about the rumors and let him deal with the matter

19. Supervisors who allow the *halo effect* to influence their evaluations of subordinates are MOST likely to

    A. give more lenient ratings to older employees who have longer service
    B. let one highly favorable or unfavorable trait unduly affect their judgment of an employee
    C. evaluate all employees on one trait before considering a second
    D. give high evaluations in order to avoid antagonizing their subordinates

20. For a supervisor to keep records of reprimands to subordinates about infractions of the rules is

    A. *good* practice, because these records are valuable to support disciplinary actions recommended or taken
    B. *poor* practice, because such records are evidence of the supervisors inability to maintain discipline
    C. *good* practice, because such records indicate that the supervisor is doing a good job
    D. *poor* practice, because the best way to correct subordinates is to give them more training

21. When a new departmental policy has been established, it would be MOST advisable for you, as a supervising agent, to

    A. distribute a memo which states the new policy and instruct your subordinates to read it
    B. explain specifically to your subordinates how the policy is going to affect them
    C. make sure your subordinates understand that you are not responsible for setting the policy
    D. tell your subordinates whether you agree or disagree with the policy

22. As a district commander, you receive several complaints about the rude conduct of an enforcement agent. The FIRST action you should take is to

   A. request his transfer to another office
   B. prepare a charge sheet for disciplinary action
   C. assign a senior agent to walk patrol with him for a week
   D. interview the agent to determine possible reason, and warn that correction is necessary

23. A supervising enforcement agent is MOST likely to get subordinates to work cooperatively toward accomplishing bureau goals if he

   A. creates an atmosphere that contributes to their feeling of security
   B. backs up subordinates even when they occasionally disobey regulations
   C. shows interest in subordinates by helping them solve their personal problems
   D. uses an authoritarian or *bossy* approach to supervision

24. A supervising agent is holding a staff meeting with his senior agents to try to find an acceptable solution to a problem that has come up.
Of the following, the CHIEF role of the supervising agent at this meeting should be to

   A. see that every member of the group contributes at least one suggestion
   B. act as chairman of the meeting, but take no other active part to avoid influencing the senior agents
   C. keep the participants from wandering off into discussions of irrelevant matters
   D. make certain the participants hear his views on the matter at the beginning of the meeting

25. An enforcement agent shows you a certificate that he has just received for completing two years of study in conversational Spanish. As his supervisor, it would be BEST for you to

   A. put a note about this accomplishment in his personnel folder
   B. assign him to areas in which people of Spanish origin live
   C. congratulate him on this accomplishment, but tell him frankly that you doubt this is likely to have any direct bearing on his work
   D. encourage him to continue his studies and become thoroughly fluent in speaking the language

KEY (CORRECT ANSWERS)

1. B
2. D
3. A
4. D
5. B

6. A
7. D
8. C
9. B
10. D

11. B
12. D
13. C
14. C
15. A

16. B
17. D
18. C
19. B
20. A

21. B
22. D
23. A
24. C
25. A

TEST 2

DIRECTIONS: Each question or incomplete statement is followed by several suggested answers or completions. Select the one that BEST answers the question or completes the statement. *PRINT THE LETTER OF THE CORRECT ANSWER IN THE SPACE AT THE RIGHT.*

1. A supervising enforcement agent is considering making a recommendation to install additional parking meters in a certain area. For this supervising agent to ask the opinion of his subordinates about the recommendation before sending it through would be

    A. *undesirable;* subordinates may lose respect for a supervisor who requests their opinions in such matters
    B. *desirable;* if additional meters are installed, it would mean more work for the subordinates, and they should have a right to help decide the matter
    C. *undesirable;* since only the supervisor would get credit for the recommendation, it would hurt the morale of the subordinates
    D. *desirable;* the subordinates may have some worthwhile suggestions concerning the recommendation

1._____

2. You have just been appointed district commander of an enforcement office new to you and overhear two of the senior enforcement agents discussing that you have a reputation for being overly strict.
The BEST action for you to take in this situation is to

    A. call the two senior agents into your office and tell them that what they heard is not true
    B. say nothing and disregard the comments since, in your position, you should be above listening to such gossip
    C. call the two senior agents into your office and caution them against spreading rumors
    D. say nothing, but use the comments you overheard for self-evaluation

2._____

3. In instructing your clerical staff on proper maintenance of the office files, you should explain that the MOST important purpose of the files is to

    A. arrange filed material so that it may be quickly found when needed
    B. prevent material from being thrown out by mistake
    C. keep written proof of actions taken so that responsibility can be assigned
    D. reduce office workload

3._____

4. Some people work safely in dangerous surroundings, whereas others have accidents on jobs that seem quite safe.
Of the following, the MOST valuable conclusion you, as a supervisor, can draw from this statement is that

    A. accident prevention depends, among other factors, upon the motivation of employees to work safely
    B. some employees are accident prone and there is nothing that can be done about it
    C. maintaining interest in safety is unnecessary if the work place and equipment are engineered for safety
    D. safety training is necessary only for certain types of employees

4._____

5. Suppose that, as a supervising enforcement agent, you have been responsible for setting up a special training program for your subordinates.
   In measuring the effectiveness of this program after it is over, it would be MOST important for you to find out

   A. whether those attending the program liked the instructor
   B. whether the objectives of the program were met and to what degree they were met
   C. whether the time involved in this training was excessive
   D. the cost to the agency for giving this training

6. Which one of the following is the most RECENT development in methods of training supervisors that involves the human relations approach?

   A. Conference training   B. Lecture method
   C. Case method   D. Sensitivity training

7. During a discussion at a staff meeting, one of your senior agents makes a statement which you know to be factually incorrect.
   If none of the other members of the group attempts to correct the statement or question it, it would be BEST for you to

   A. allow the discussion to continue without commenting
   B. correct the statement that has been made
   C. emphasize that statements made at the meeting by members of the group are not to be accepted as fact
   D. urge the group to decide for themselves whether or not to accept the statement that was made

8. For a supervisor to give his subordinates oral as well as written instructions on work that is detailed or complex is

   A. *desirable,* because it would give subordinates an overall view of the particular job and its relation to the agencys goals
   B. *undesirable,* because this would discourage initiative on the part of subordinates
   C. *desirable,* because the supervisor can find out if subordinates understand the written instructions and answer any questions they have
   D. *undesirable,* because subordinates should be able to work efficiently from the written instructions if they are complete

9. The lecture-demonstration method would be LEAST desirable in a training program set up for

   A. breaking in new employees
   B. changing the attitudes of older employees
   C. explaining how a new piece of equipment works
   D. informing subordinates about new agency procedures

10. The MAIN reason for having the department of traffic give out publicity about the work of the bureau of enforcement is to

    A. justify increased money for the department in future city budgets
    B. show the public the need for better salaries for employees of this very important bureau

C. free the top officials of the department from the pressures of special interest groups
D. inform the public about the work and problems of this bureau so that they will better understand and comply with its regulations

11. Suppose one of your agents was in an accident while on patrol. Two days later a man who says he is a newspaper reporter wants to interview you about what happened.
It would be MOST advisable for you to tell him that

    A. he must speak to the senior agent who saw the accident
    B. you cannot give him any information because he may misquote you
    C. he must contact the main office of the department of traffic for official information
    D. the accident was not serious and is not worth reporting in the newspaper

11.____

12. While you are checking an area, a motorist in a private car complains to you that an agent issued a summons to him for double parking but that a passenger car parked right behind him did not get a summons.
The BEST action for you to take is to tell him

    A. to give you all the information and you will investigate the matter
    B. to call the main office
    C. that it was probably just an oversight and you will speak to the agent
    D. that whether or not the other driver got a summons is not his business

12.____

13. Suppose you receive a letter from a man who complains that he was treated rudely by one of your enforcement agents.
Of the following, the FIRST action you should take is to

    A. write a letter of apology to the man for the enforcement agents discourtesy
    B. disregard the complaint because this agent is known to be courteous at all times
    C. obtain all details of the incident from the enforcement agent
    D. forward the letter to the director of the bureau of enforcement

13.____

14. When a supervising agent speaks over the phone to members of the public who have questions or complaints, it is MOST important that what he says should

    A. please the caller
    B. give a good impression of the speaker
    C. be as brief as possible
    D. conform to bureau policies

14.____

15. When you are training new enforcement agents, you should instruct them that if a motorist is loud and rude to then they should

    A. shout right back in the same manner
    B. call a policeman and have the motorist arrested
    C. say nothing and continue on patrol
    D. hide their badge and refuse to give their number

15.____

16. Of the following, the LEAST important reason for having a department handbook and a bureau standard operating procedure is to

    A. help in training new employees
    B. provide a source of reference for department and bureau rules and procedures

16.____

C. prevent errors in work by providing clear guidelines
D. make the supervisors job easy

17. A Form 15 must be submitted by an employee of the bureau of enforcement for any absence EXCEPT

    A. a civil service job interview
    B. vacation days listed on the approved annual leave schedule
    C. emergency leave
    D. time off for overtime

17.____

18. Suppose you get a flat tire at 3:00 P.M. while on tour in a department vehicle. The CORRECT action you should take is to

    A. ask the communications center to send the A.A.A.
    B. leave the car at the curb and phone the district office
    C. use a local garage to fix the flat and get a bill in duplicate
    D. use the car radio to call the department shop for assistance

18.____

19. One of your enforcement agents is reporting a high number of summons refusals. Of the following, the MOST effective way for you to handle the situation is to

    A. give the agent an unsatisfactory performance evaluation
    B. provide for retraining of the agent
    C. arrange to have the agent reassigned to another district office
    D. refer the matter to the principal enforcement agent

19.____

20. A supervisor is giving instructions to the agents under his supervision on the proper procedures to follow if assaulted while on patrol. Which one of the following statements should NOT be made by the supervisor to his subordinates?

    A. Make a citizen's arrest of the assailant.
    B. Obtain police assistance, if required.
    C. Notify the district commander.
    D. Obtain medical care if necessary.

20.____

21. When a supervising agent has been informed of summonses lost before being served, he should IMMEDIATELY notify the

    A. traffic summons control bureau
    B. parking violations bureau
    C. police department
    D. criminal court

21.____

22. A parking enforcement agent has been late 8 times in January, 2 times in February, and 6 times in March.
As the supervising agent, the CORRECT action for you to take is to

    A. refer the matter to the deputy commissioner for administration
    B. speak to the agent, emphasizing the need for promptness
    C. direct the senior enforcement agent to issue a below-standard performance evaluation for this agent
    D. arrange an appointment for the agent to speak with the bureau chief

22.____

23. A senior enforcement agent reports to the district commander that, on inspecting his squad prior to patrol, he has noted an agent improperly and unacceptably uniformed, and correction cannot be made immediately.
The district commander should properly

    A. send the agent home and authorize no pay for the day
    B. permit the agent to proceed on patrol, but warn him not to let this happen again
    C. assign the agent to clerical work for the day
    D. notify the principal enforcement agent right away

24. Of the following, the factor MOST likely to cause lowered morale among enforcement agents is

    A. lack of higher salaries
    B. necessity for working rotating shifts
    C. abuse from citizens whom they have summoned
    D. working in *paired* areas

25. In determining whether an agent is issuing a satisfactory number of summonses while on patrol, the supervisor should

    A. set a daily summons quota and compare the agents record against this figure
    B. take into consideration previous records of summonses issued in the areas patrolled by the agent
    C. consider that the agent is doing satisfactory work if there are no complaints about him
    D. consider the attitudes and personality of the agent rather than the number of summonses he issues

---

KEY (CORRECT ANSWERS)

1. D		11. C
2. D		12. A
3. A		13. C
4. A		14. D
5. B		15. C
6. D		16. D
7. B		17. B
8. C		18. C
9. B		19. B
10. D		20. A

21. C
22. D
23. A
24. C
25. B

EXAMINATION SECTION
TEST 1

DIRECTIONS: Each question or incomplete statement is followed by several suggested answers or completions. Select the one that BEST answers the question or completes the statement. *PRINT THE LETTER OF THE CORRECT ANSWER IN THE SPACE AT THE RIGHT.*

1. An employee of the bureau who has used up all his sick leave submits a form requesting that a Monday absence be changed to sick leave.
   The MOST appropriate action for the district commander to take is to

   A. recommend that the absence be charged *Sick - No Pay*
   B. recommend that the absence be charged to annual leave
   C. approve a request for advance sick time to be prepared by the employee
   D. forward the employee's form without approval

   1.____

2. Unless exempted by administrative direction, it is a policy of the bureau of enforcement that all records, other than summons stubs and field patrol reports, are to be

   A. kept indefinitely
   B. destroyed after three years
   C. destroyed after five years
   D. destroyed only when directed

   2.____

3. The collection of parking meter funds is the responsibility of the

   A. transportation administration
   B. comptroller's office
   C. finance administration
   D. municipal services administration

   3.____

4. If a citizen accuses an enforcement agent on patrol of damaging his car, the agent should tell him to make his complaint to the

   A. office of the comptroller
   B. main office of the department of traffic
   C. police department
   D. finance administration

   4.____

5. The 6:30 A.M. - 2:30 P.M. tour is always scheduled from Monday through Friday because

   A. the inconvenient hours deserve a bonus of weekends off
   B. the Police Department is able to give more time to enforcement of traffic regulations on Saturday mornings
   C. an important traffic regulation to be enforced is in effect from Monday through Friday only
   D. cars are not available on Saturday

   5.____

6. If a supervising enforcement agent feels there are reasons why it would be desirable to change patrols in order to cover an area not previously patrolled, he should

   6.____

13

A. recommend the change to the principal enforcement agent after consulting with the senior agents
B. have the senior agents submit written reports on the desirability of the change
C. conduct a 30-day test of the proposed patrol
D. send a memorandum to the main office of the bureau

7. You are operating a department vehicle with the two-way radio on. As you approach a construction site, you see a posted warning that blasting is in progress. According to standard operating procedure of the bureau of enforcement, the CORRECT action for you to take is to

    A. immediately turn off the radio
    B. report the exact location of the blasting area to the communications center
    C. keep the radio on, but not use the microphone
    D. leave the neighborhood of the construction site at once

8. If meters are to be installed in an area where four banks are located, the MOST suitable type to use would be _____ hour meters.

    A. 1/2   B. 1   C. 2   D. 3

9. The parking violations bureau requires that summonses forwarded to them be separated according to

    A. violation codes
    B. make of the vehicles
    C. type of registration of the vehicles
    D. police precincts in which the violations occurred

10. The flashing red signal on a traffic light has basically the same meaning for motorists as a

    A. steady yellow signal on a traffic light
    B. yield sign
    C. stop sign
    D. red arrow signal on a traffic light

11. The settlement of all traffic offenses formerly handled by the Criminal Court is now shared by the Transportation Administration (PVB) and the

    A. State Department of Motor Vehicles
    B. Criminal Court
    C. Police Department plus the State Department of Motor Vehicles
    D. State Department of Motor Vehicles plus the Criminal Court

12. The penalties that can be imposed for a violation of traffic rules and regulations in the city are set forth in the

    A. City Charter
    B. State Vehicle and Traffic Law
    C. Administrative Code
    D. City Traffic Regulations

13. Parking summonses are NOT issued by the 13.____

    A. Bureau of Franchises
    B. Fire Department
    C. Port Authority
    D. Department of Highways

14. Which one of these is NOT a part of the Transportation Administration? 14.____

    A. Department of Highways
    B. Department of Marine and Aviation
    C. Department of Traffic
    D. Triborough Bridge and Tunnel Authority

15. All moving violations of traffic regulations in the city are handled by the 15.____

    A. Transportation Administration (PVB)
    B. State Department of Motor Vehicles (Administrative Adjudication Bureau)
    C. Criminal Court
    D. Traffic Court

16. The MOST widely used type of safety warning signs manufactured by the traffic department's bureau of signs and markings are the _____ signs. 16.____

    A. school crossing
    B. lane-squeeze
    C. curve
    D. turn

Questions 17-22.

DIRECTIONS: Questions 17 through 22 are to be answered ONLY according to the information given in the paragraph below.

Perhaps the strongest argument the mass transit backer has is the advantage in efficiency that mass transit has over the automobile in the urban traffic picture. It has been estimated that given comparable location and construction conditions, the subway can carry four times as many passengers per hour and cost half as much to build as urban highways. Yet public apathy regarding the mass transportation movement in the 1960's resulted in the building of more roads. Planned to provide 42,000 miles of highways in the period from 1956-72, including 7500 miles within cities, the Federal Highway System project is now about two-thirds completed. The Highway Trust Fund supplies 90 percent of the cost of the System, with state and local-sources putting up the rest of the money. By contrast, a municipality has had to put up the bulk of the cost of a rapid transit system. Although the System and its Trust Fund have come under attack in the past few years from environmentalists and groups opposed to the continued building of urban freeways - considered to be the most expensive, destructive, and inefficient segments of the System - a move by them to get the Trust Fund transformed into a general transportation fund at the expiration of the present program seems to be headed nowhere.

17. Given similar building conditions and location, a city that builds a subway instead of a highway can expect to receive for each dollar spent _____ as much transport value. 17.____

    A. half
    B. twice
    C. four times
    D. eight times

18. The general attitude of the public in the past ten years toward the mass transportation movement has been

   A. favorable
   B. indifferent
   C. enthusiastic
   D. unfriendly

19. The number of miles of highways still to be completed in the Federal Highway System project is MOST NEARLY

   A. 2,500   B. 5,000   C. 14,000   D. 28,000

20. What do certain groups who object to some features of the Federal Highway System program want to do with the Highway Trust Fund after its expiration date?

   A. Extend it in order to complete the project
   B. Change it so that the money can be used for all types of transportation
   C. End it even if the project is not completed
   D. Change it so that the money will be used only for urban freeways

21. Which one of the following statements is a valid conclusion based on the facts in the above passage?

   A. The advantage of greater efficiency is the only argument that supporters of the mass transportation movement can offer.
   B. It was easier for cities to build roads rather than mass transit systems in the last 15 years because of the large financial contribution made by the Federal government.
   C. Mass transit systems cause as much congestion and air pollution in cities as automobiles.
   D. The Highway Trust Fund will become a general transportation fund.

22. The MAIN idea or theme of the above passage is that the

   A. cost of the Federal Highway System is shared by the federal, state, and local governments
   B. public is against spending money for building mass transportation facilities in the cities
   C. cities would benefit more from expansion and improvement of their mass transit systems than from the building of more highways
   D. building of mass transportation facilities has been slowed by the Highway Trust Fund

23. To which one of the following problems should you, as a supervising agent, give LOWEST priority during a very busy work period?

   A. A letter of complaint from an angry citizen has been referred from the mayor's office.
   B. The director of the bureau wants you to investigate and report on the advisability of introducing a new filing system at some future date.
   C. The senior enforcement agents have a grievance they wish to discuss with you.
   D. An agent has violated a departmental rule and disciplinary action is required.

24. Of the following duties of a supervising enforcement agent, the one that it would be LEAST desirable to delegate to a senior enforcement agent is

    A. contacting local police precincts for information
    B. checking of records on which reports to superiors are based
    C. speaking to enforcement agents about some new department regulations
    D. reorganization of office and field staff

25. During a certain three-month period, the bureau of enforcement issued 239,788 summonses. Of these, 37,900 were issued between the hours of 12 Noon and 1 P.M.; 33,350 were issued between 1 P.M. and 2 P.M.; and 23,334 were issued between 2 P.M. and 3 P.M.
    What percentage of the total number of summonses issued during this three-month period was issued between 1 P.M. and 3 P.M.?

    A. 22%   B. 24%   C. 26%   D. 28%

KEY (CORRECT ANSWERS)

1. A		11. D	
2. B		12. A	
3. C		13. D	
4. A		14. D	
5. C		15. B	
6. A		16. A	
7. C		17. D	
8. A		18. B	
9. D		19. C	
10. C		20. B	

21. B
22. C
23. B
24. D
25. B

TEST 2

DIRECTIONS: Each question or incomplete statement is followed by several suggested answers or completions. Select the one that BEST answers the question or completes the statement. *PRINT THE LETTER OF THE CORRECT ANSWER IN THE SPACE AT THE RIGHT.*

Questions 1-6.

DIRECTIONS: Questions 1 through 6 are to be answered SOLELY on the basis of the information given in the paragraph below.

The use of role-playing as a training technique was developed during the past decade by social scientists, particularly psychologists, who have been active in training experiments. Originally, this technique was applied by clinical psychologists who discovered that a patient appears to gain understanding of an emotionally disturbing situation when encouraged to act out roles in that situation. As applied in government and business organizations, the purpose of role-playing is to aid employees to understand certain work problems involving interpersonal relations and to enable observers to evaluate various reactions to them. Thus, for example, on the problem of handling grievances, two individuals from the group might be selected to act out extemporaneously the parts of subordinate and supervisor. When this situation is enacted by various pairs among the class and the techniques and results are discussed, the members of the group are presumed to reach conclusions about the most effective means of handling similar situations. Often the use of role reversal, where participants take parts different from their actual work roles, assists individuals to gain more insight into other people's problems and viewpoints. Although role-playing can be a rewarding training device, the trainer must be aware of his responsibilities. If this technique is to be successful, thorough briefing of both actors and observers as to the situation in question, the participants' roles, and what to look for, is essential.

1. The role-playing technique was FIRST used for the purpose of 1.___
    A. measuring the effectiveness of training programs
    B. training supervisors in business organizations
    C. treating emotionally disturbed patients
    D. handling employee grievances

2. When role-playing is used in private business as a training device, the CHIEF aim is to 2.___
    A. develop better relations between supervisor and subordinate in the handling of grievances
    B. come up with a solution to a specific problem that has arisen
    C. determine the training needs of the group
    D. increase employee understanding of the human relation factors in work situations

3. From the above passage, it is MOST reasonable to conclude that when role-playing is used, it is preferable to have the roles acted out by 3.___
    A. only one set of actors
    B. no more than two sets of actors
    C. several different sets of actors
    D. the trainer or trainers of the group

4. Based on the above passage, a trainer using the technique of role reversal in a problem of first-line supervision should assign a senior enforcement agent to play the part of a(n)

   A. enforcement agent
   B. senior enforcement agent
   C. principal enforcement agent
   D. angry citizen

4.____

5. It can be inferred from the above passage that a *limitation* of role-play as a training method is that

   A. many work situations do not lend themselves to role-play
   B. employees are not experienced enough as actors to play the roles realistically
   C. only trainers who have psychological training can use it successfully
   D. participants who are observing and not acting do not benefit from it

5.____

6. To obtain good results from the use of role-play in training, a trainer should give participants

   A. a minimum of information about the situation so that they can act spontaneously
   B. scripts which illustrate the best method for handling the situation
   C. a complete explanation of the problem and the roles to be acted out
   D. a summary of work problems which involve interpersonal relations

6.____

7. Of the following, the MOST important reason for a supervisor to prepare *good* written reports is that

   A. a supervisor is rated on the quality of his reports
   B. decisions are often made on the basis of the reports
   C. such reports take less time for superiors to review
   D. such reports demonstrate efficiency of department operations

7.____

8. Of the following, the BEST test of a *good* report is whether it

   A. provides the information needed
   B. shows the good sense of the writer
   C. is prepared according to a proper format
   D. is grammatical and neat

8.____

9. When a supervisor writes a report, he can BEST show that he has an understanding of the subject of the report by

   A. including necessary facts and omitting non-essential details
   B. using statistical data
   C. giving his conclusions but not the data on which they are based
   D. using a technical vocabulary

9.____

10. Suppose you and another supervisor on the same level are assigned to work together on a report. You disagree strongly with one of the recommendations the other supervisor wants to include in the report but you cannot change his views.
    Of the following, it would be BEST that

    A. you refuse to accept responsibility for the report
    B. you ask that someone else be assigned to this project to replace you

10.____

C. each of you state his own ideas about this recommendation in the report
D. you give in to the other supervisor's opinion for the sake of harmony

11. Standardized forms are often provided for submitting reports.
Of the following, the MOST important advantage of using standardized forms for reports is that

    A. they take less time to prepare than individually written reports
    B. necessary information is less likely to be omitted
    C. the responsibility for preparing these reports can be delegated to subordinates
    D. the person making the report can omit information he considers unimportant

12. A report which may BEST be classed as a *periodic* report is one which

    A. requires the same type of information at regular intervals
    B. contains detailed information which is to be retained in permanent records
    C. is prepared whenever a special situation occurs
    D. lists information in graphic form

13. Which one of the following is NOT an important reason for keeping accurate records in an office?

    A. Facts will be on hand when decisions have to be made.
    B. The basis for past actions can be determined.
    C. Information needed by other bureaus can be furnished.
    D. Filing is easier when records are properly made out.

14. Suppose you are preparing to write a report recommending a change in a certain procedure. You learn that another supervisor made a report a few years ago suggesting a change in this same procedure, but that no action was taken.
Of the following, it would be MOST desirable for you to

    A. avoid reading the other supervisor's report, so that you will write with a more up-to-date point of view
    B. make no recommendation, since management seems to be against any change in the procedure
    C. read the other report before you write your report, to see what bearing it may have on your recommendations
    D. avoid including in your report any information that can be obtained by referring to the other report

15. If a report you are preparing to your superior is going to be a very long one, it would be DESIRABLE to include a summary of your basic conclusions

    A. at the end of the report
    B. at the beginning of the report
    C. in a separate memorandum
    D. right after you present the supporting data

16. Suppose that some bureau and department policies must be very frequently applied by your subordinates while others rarely come into use.
    As a supervising enforcement agent, a GOOD technique for you to use in fulfilling your responsibility of seeing to it that policies are adhered to is to

    A. ask the director of the bureau to issue to all employees an explanation in writing of all policies
    B. review with your subordinates every week those policies which have daily application
    C. follow up on and explain at regular intervals the application of those policies which are not used very often by your subordinates
    D. recommend to your superiors that policies rarely used be changed or dropped

17. The BASIC purpose behind the principle of delegation of authority is to

    A. give the supervisor who is delegating a chance to acquire skills in higher level functions
    B. free the supervisor from routine tasks in order that he may do the important parts of his job
    C. prevent supervisors from overstepping the lines of authority which have been established
    D. place the work delegated in the hands of those employees who can perform it best

18. A district commander can BEST assist management in long-range planning for the bureau of enforcement by

    A. reporting to his superiors any changing conditions in the district
    B. maintaining a neat and efficiently run office
    C. scheduling patrols so that areas with a high rate of non-compliance get more intensive coverage
    D. properly training new personnel assigned to his district

19. Suppose that new quarters have been rented for your district office.
    Of the following, the LEAST important factor to be considered in planning the layout of the office is the

    A. need for screening confidential activities from unauthorized persons
    B. relative importance of the various types of work
    C. areas of noise concentration
    D. convenience with which communication between sections of the office can be achieved

20. Of the following, the MOST basic effect of organizing a department so that lines of authority are clearly defined and duties are specifically assigned is to

    A. increase the need for close supervision
    B. decrease the initiative of subordinates
    C. lessen the possibility of duplication of work
    D. increase the responsibilities of supervisory personnel

21. An accepted management principle is that decisions should be delegated to the lowest point in the organization at which they can be made effectively.
The one of the following which is MOST likely to be a result of the application of this principle is that

    A. no factors will be overlooked in making decisions
    B. prompt action will follow the making of decisions
    C. decisions will be made more rapidly
    D. coordination of decisions that are made will be simplified

22. Suppose you are a supervisor and need some guidance from a higher authority.
In which one of the following situations would it be PERMISSIBLE for you to bypass the regular upward channels of communication in the chain of command?

    A. In an emergency when your superior is not available
    B. When it is not essential to get a quick reply
    C. When you feel your immediate superior is not understanding of the situation
    D. When you want to obtain information that you think your superior does not have

23. Of the following, the CHIEF limitation of the organization chart as it is generally used in business and government is that the chart

    A. makes lines of responsibility and authority undesirably definite and formal
    B. is often out of date as soon as it is completed
    C. does not show human factors and informal working relationships
    D. is usually too complicated

24. The *span of control* for any supervisor is the

    A. *number* of tasks he is expected to perform himself
    B. *total* office space he and his subordinates occupy
    C. *amount* of work he is responsible for getting out
    D. *number* of subordinates he can supervise effectively

25. Of the following duties performed by a supervising enforcement agent, which would be considered a LINE function rather than a STAFF function?

    A. Evaluation of office personnel
    B. Recommendations for disciplinary action
    C. Initiating budget requests for replacement of equipment
    D. Inspections, at irregular times, of conditions and staff in the field

KEY (CORRECT ANSWERS)

1. C
2. D
3. C
4. A
5. A

6. C
7. B
8. A
9. A
10. C

11. B
12. A
13. D
14. C
15. B

16. C
17. B
18. A
19. B
20. C

21. B
22. A
23. C
24. D
25. D

EXAMINATION SECTION
TEST 1

DIRECTIONS: Each question or incomplete statement is followed by several suggested answers or completions. Select the one that BEST answers the question or completes the statement. *PRINT THE LETTER OF THE CORRECT ANSWER IN THE SPACE AT THE RIGHT.*

1. Of the following, the factor affecting employee morale which the immediate supervisor is LEAST able to control is

    A. handling of grievances
    B. fair and impartial treatment of subordinates
    C. general personnel rules and regulations
    D. accident prevention

1.____

2. When one of your agents does outstanding work, you should

    A. explain to your other agents that you expect the same kind of work from them
    B. praise him for his work so that he will know it is appreciated
    C. say nothing because other agents may think you are showing favoritism
    D. show him how his work can be improved even more so that he will not sit back

2.____

3. For you as a supervisor to consider a suggestion from a probationary agent for improving a procedure would be

    A. *poor* practice, because this agent is too new on the job to know much about it
    B. *good* practice, because you may be able to share credit for the suggestion
    C. *poor* practice, because it may hurt the morale of the older employees
    D. *good* practice, because the suggestion may be worthwhile

3.____

4. If you find you must criticize the work of one of your enforcement agents, it would be BEST for you to

    A. mention the good points in his work as well as the faults
    B. caution him that he will receive an unsatisfactory performance report unless his work improves
    C. compare his work to that of the other agents you supervise
    D. apologize for making the criticism

4.____

5. As a senior enforcement agent, which one of the following matters would it be BEST for you to talk over with your supervisor before you take final action?

    A. One of the agents you supervise continues to disregard your instructions repeatedly in spite of repeated warnings.
    B. One of your agents tells you he wants to discuss a personal problem.
    C. A probationary agent tells you he does not understand a procedure.
    D. One of your agents tells you he disagrees with the way you rate his work.

5.____

6. If one of your subordinates asks you a question about a department rule and you do not know the answer, you should tell him that

    A. he should try to get the information himself
    B. you do not have the answer, but you will get it for him as soon as you can

6.____

C. he should ask you the question again a week from now
D. he should put the question in writing

7. If, as a senior agent, you realize that you have been unfair in criticizing one of your subordinates, the BEST action for you to take is to

   A. say nothing but overlook some error made by this agent in the future
   B. be frank and tell the agent that you are sorry for the mistake you made
   C. let the agent know in some indirect way, without admitting your mistake, that you realize he was not at fault
   D. say nothing but be more careful about criticizing subordinates in the future

8. Of the following, the MOST important reason for a supervisor to write an accident report as soon as possible after an accident has happened is to

   A. make sure that important facts about the accident are not forgotten
   B. avoid delay in getting compensation for the injured person
   C. get adequate medical treatment for the injured person
   D. keep department accident statistics up to date

9. In any matter which may require disciplinary action, the FIRST responsibility of the supervisor is to

   A. decide what penalty should be applied for the offense
   B. refer the matter to a higher authority for complete investigation
   C. place the interests of the department above those of the employee
   D. investigate the matter fully to get all the facts

10. Suppose you find it necessary to criticize one of the enforcement agents you supervise. You should

    A. send an official letter to his home
    B. speak to him about the matter privately
    C. speak to him at a staff meeting
    D. ask another enforcement agent who is friendly with him to talk to him about the matter

11. Some of your subordinates have been coming to you with complaints you feel are unimportant.
    For you to hear their stories out is

    A. *poor* practice; you should spend your time on more important matters
    B. *good* practice; this will increase your popularity with your subordinates
    C. *poor* practice; subordinates should learn to come to you only with major grievances
    D. *good* practice; it may prevent minor complaints from developing into major grievances

12. Suppose that not one of a group of employees has turned in an idea to the employees' suggestion system during the past year.
    The MOST probable reason for this situation is that the

A. supervisor of these employees is not doing enough to encourage them to take part in this program
B. employees in this group are not able to develop any good ideas
C. money awards given for suggestions used are not high enough to make employees interested
D. methods and procedures of operation do not need improvement

13. For you as a supervisor to give each of your subordinates *exactly the same* type of supervision is

    A. *advisable,* because doing this insures fair and impartial treatment of each individual
    B. *not advisable,* because each person is different and there is no one supervisory procedure for dealing with individuals that applies in every case
    C. *advisable,* because once a supervisor learns how to deal with a subordinate who brings a problem to him, he can handle another subordinate with this problem in the same way
    D. *not advisable,* because individuals like to think that they are receiving better treatment than others

14. In evaluating personnel, a supervisor should keep in mind that the MOST important objective of performance evaluations is to

    A. encourage employees to compete for higher performance ratings
    B. give recognition to employees who perform well
    C. help employees improve their work
    D. discipline employees who perform poorly

15. A subordinate tells you that he is having trouble concentrating on his work due to a personal problem at home.
    Of the following, it would be BEST for you to

    A. refer him to a community service agency
    B. listen quietly to the story, because he may just need a sympathetic ear
    C. tell him that you cannot help him because the problem is not job-related
    D. ask him some questions about the nature of the problem and tell him how you would handle it

16. To do a good job of performance evaluation, it is BEST for a supervisor to

    A. measure the employee's performance against standard performance requirements
    B. compare the employee's performance to that of another employee doing similar work
    C. leave out any consideration of the employee's personal traits
    D. give greatest weight to instances of unusually good or unusually poor performance

17. It is particularly important that disciplinary actions be equitable as between individuals.
    This statement implies that

    A. punishment applied in disciplinary actions should be lenient
    B. proposed disciplinary actions should be reviewed by higher authority

C. subordinates should have an opportunity to present their stories before penalties are applied
D. penalties for violations of the rules should be standardized and consistently applied

18. Assume that an agency has an established procedure for handling employee grievances. An employee in this agency comes to his immediate supervisor with a grievance. The supervisor investigates the matter and makes a decision. However, the employee is not satisfied with the decision made by the supervisor.
The BEST action for the supervisor to take is to

    A. tell the employee he will review the matter further
    B. remind the employee that he is the supervisor and the employee must act in accordance with his decision
    C. explain to the employee how he can carry his complaint forward to the next step in the grievance procedure
    D. tell the employee he will consult with his own superiors on the matter

19. Of the following, the CHIEF purpose of a probationary period for a new employee is to allow time for

    A. finding out whether the selection processes are satisfactory
    B. determining the fitness of the employee to continue in the job
    C. the employee to decide whether he wants a permanent appointment
    D. the employee to make adjustments in his home circumstances made necessary by the job

20. Of the following, the subject that would be LEAST important to include in a *break-in* program for new enforcement agents is

    A. explanation of rules, regulations, and policies of the agency
    B. instruction in the agency's history and programs
    C. explanation of the importance of the new employees' own particular job
    D. explanation of the duties and responsibilities of the parking meter collectors who collect the parking meter fees

21. Suppose a new enforcement agent under your supervision seems slow to learn and is making mistakes in writing summonses.
Your FIRST action should be to

    A. pass this information on to the district commander
    B. reprimand the agent so he will not repeat these mistakes
    C. find out whether this agent understands your instructions
    D. note these facts for future reference when writing up the monthly performance evaluation

22. In training new enforcement agents to do a certain job, it would be LEAST desirable for you to

    A. demonstrate how the job is done, step by step
    B. encourage the agents to ask questions if they aren't clear about any point
    C. tell them about the various mistakes other agents have made in doing this job
    D. have the agents do the job, explaining to you what they are doing and why

23. One of the agents under your supervision is resentful when you ask her to remove her jangling bracelets before she starts on patrol.
    Of the following, the BEST explanation you can give her for the rule against wearing such jewelry while on duty is that

    A. the jewelry may create a safety hazard
    B. employees must give up certain personal liberties if they want to keep their jobs
    C. agents cannot perform their duties as efficiently if they wear distracting jewelry
    D. citizens may receive an unfavorable impression of the department

24. Of the following, the LEAST important reason for having a department handbook and a bureau standard operating procedure is to

    A. help in training new employees
    B. provide a source of reference for department and bureau rules and procedures
    C. prevent errors in work by providing clear guidelines
    D. make the supervisor's job easy

25. On inspecting your squad prior to patrol, you note an enforcement agent improperly and unacceptably uniformed. The FIRST action you should take is to

    A. call the enforcement agent aside and insist on immediate correction if possible
    B. notify the district commander right away
    C. have the enforcement agent submit a memorandum explaining the reason for the improper uniform
    D. permit the enforcement agent to proceed on patrol but warn him not to let this happen again

KEY (CORRECT ANSWERS)

1.	C	11.	D
2.	B	12.	A
3.	D	13.	B
4.	A	14.	C
5.	A	15.	B
6.	B	16.	A
7.	B	17.	D
8.	A	18.	C
9.	D	19.	B
10.	B	20.	D

21. C
22. C
23. D
24. D
25. A

TEST 2

DIRECTIONS: Each question or incomplete statement is followed by several suggested answers or completions. Select the one that BEST answers the question or completes the statement. *PRINT THE LETTER OF THE CORRECT ANSWER IN THE SPACE AT THE RIGHT.*

1. An enforcement agent is just preparing to write a summons for double parking when the driver of the vehicle returns to nove the car.
   For this enforcement agent to continue on patrol without issuing the summons is

   A. *advisable,* since he had not started to write the summons and, therefore, should extend this courtesy to the citizen
   B. *inadvisable,* since it is the agent's duty to issue the summons
   C. *advisable,* since the driver may abuse or assault him if he issues the summons
   D. *inadvisable,* since it may lead the driver to think he can get away with other parking violations

   1.____

2. For enforcement agents on duty to give street directions to the public when asked for them is

   A. *good* practice, because the agents are best qualified to know all the streets in their district
   B. *poor* practice, because this may delay them in covering their assigned areas fully
   C. *good* practice, because this helps to establish a good relationship between the public and the department
   D. *poor* practice, because police officers are better qualified to give such information

   2.____

3. The MAIN reason for having the department of traffic give out publicity about the work of the bureau of enforcement is to

   A. justify increased money for the department in future budgets
   B. show the public the need for better salaries for employees of this very important bureau
   C. free the top officials of the department from the pressures of special interest groups
   D. inform the public about the work and problems of this bureau so that they will better understand and comply with its regulations

   3.____

4. When you are training new enforcement agents, you should instruct them that if a motorist is loud and rude to them, they should

   A. say nothing and continue on patrol
   B. call a policeman and have the motorist arrested
   C. shout right back in the same manner
   D. hide their badge and refuse to give their number

   4.____

5. While you are checking an area, a motorist in a private car complains to you that an agent issued a summons to him for double parking but that a passenger car parked right behind him did not get a summons.
   The BEST action for you to take is to tell him

   5.____

30

A. to call the main office
B. to give you all the information and you will investigate the matter
C. that it was probably just an oversight and you will speak to the agent
D. that whether or not the other driver got a summons is not his business

6. Rules of the bureau of enforcement require that summonses are to be issued for parking violations even when

   A. there is no sign
   B. the vehicles are fire engines or ambulances
   C. the car has DPL plates
   D. the car has a PBA card

7. When a plate number on a state permit and the plate on the car do not agree, the enforcement agent should

   A. notify the district commander to advise the state office
   B. report the matter to the state office immediately by phone
   C. note all the information on the appropriate form
   D. notify the bureau chief at the main office

8. On checking your patrol, you find one of your agents off-post. Your FIRST action should be to

   A. reprimand him and send him to his proper post
   B. prepare a memorandum to the district commander
   C. ask the agent to prepare a memorandum
   D. enter the incident on his form and on yours

9. What is the CORRECT procedure an enforcement agent should follow to report a defective off-street meter?

   A. Report on Optical Scanning Card
   B. Report on the appropriate form
   C. Make note on summons
   D. Make an oral report to the senior agent

10. When an agent on patrol observes a vehicle on violation on the opposite side of the street, he should

    A. cross immediately and issue a summons
    B. walk to the nearest crosswalk and go back to issue the summons
    C. continue on patrol
    D. note violation on the appropriate form

11. A parking privilege extended to a driver displaying an SVI card is permission to park

    A. at meters free   B. in No Standing areas
    C. at bus stops   D. in DPL spaces

12. If an enforcement agent sees a badly damaged on-street meter, the CORRECT procedure for the agent to follow is to

    A. note the location of the meter on the appropriate form
    B. prepare an Optical Scanning Card and submit it on return from patrol

C. ignore it since damaged meters are common and are not within the range of an agent's duties
D. make a note and call the main office

13. Form Enf. 63 should be used by enforcement agents to report

    A. defective on-street meters
    B. lost summonses
    C. summons refusals
    D. possible stolen vehicles

14. From the enforcement agent's viewpoint, the MOST important result of the establishment of the parking violations bureau is that

    A. enforcement is more rapid and efficient
    B. agents rarely have had to testify on tickets issued since
    C. collection of fines has been speeded up
    D. policemen are able to devote more of their time to fighting crime

15. Double parking is permitted by any

    A. commercial vehicle that is quickly loading or unloading alongside a curb where parking is permitted
    B. vehicle with a person at the wheel
    C. vehicle that is quickly loading or unloading
    D. vehicle with MD plates

16. Unmarked police cars displaying green or blue enameled plaques should be tagged only when

    A. parked at a meter on violation
    B. parked at a hydrant
    C. parked in a bus stop
    D. double parked

17. Foreign consuls are issued distinctive license plates which include the letters FC. Which one of the following is a foreign consul plate?

    A. 1237 FC   B. FC 1237   C. 12 FC 37   D. 9 FCA

18. Which of the following is a Sunday holiday according to city traffic regulations?

    A. Lincoln's Birthday   B. Labor Day
    C. Columbus Day   D. Veterans' Day

19. While checking the agency copies of summonses, you discover that part of the serial number is missing on one summons.
    The CORRECT action for you to take is to

    A. notify the district commander
    B. destroy the copy and make out another
    C. determine the correct number and insert it in ink
    D. have the enforcement agent prepare a memorandum of explanation

20. A form must be submitted by an employee of the bureau of enforcement for any absence EXCEPT

    A. a city civil service job interview
    B. vacation days listed on the approved annual leave schedule
    C. emergency leave
    D. time off for overtime

21. Suppose you get a flat tire at 3:00 P.M. while on tour in a department vehicle. The CORRECT action you should take is to

    A. ask the communications center to send the A.A.A.
    B. leave the car at the curb and phone the district office
    C. use a local garage to fix the flat and get a bill in duplicate
    D. use the car radio to call the department for assistance

22. A supervisor is giving instructions to the agents under his supervision on the proper procedures to follow if assaulted while on patrol.
    Which one of the following statements should NOT be made by the supervisor to his subordinates?

    A. Make a citizen's arrest of the assailant
    B. Obtain police assistance, if required
    C. Notify the district commander
    D. Obtain medical care if necessary

23. The 6:30 A.M. - 2:30 P.M. tour is always scheduled from Monday through Friday because

    A. the inconvenient hours deserve a bonus of weekends off
    B. the Police Department is able to give more time to enforcement of traffic regulations on Saturday mornings
    C. an important traffic regulation to be enforced is in effect from Monday through Friday only
    D. cars are not available on Saturday

24. You are operating a department vehicle with the two-way radio on. As you approach a construction site, you see a posted warning that blasting is in progress.
    According to standard operating procedure of the bureau of enforcement, the CORRECT action for you to take is to

    A. immediately turn off the radio
    B. report the exact location of the blasting area to the communications center
    C. keep the radio on, but not use the microphone
    D. leave the neighborhood of the construction site at once

25. Of the following, the factor MOST likely to cause lowered morale among enforcement agents is

    A. lack of higher salaries
    B. necessity for working rotating shifts
    C. abuse from citizens whom they have summonsed
    D. working in *paired* areas

26. If a citizen accuses an enforcement agent on patrol of damaging his car, the agent should tell him to make his complaint to the

   A. finance administration
   B. main office of the department of traffic
   C. police department
   D. office of the comptrolle

27. The parking violations bureau requires that summonses forwarded to them be separated according to

   A. violation codes
   B. make of the vehicles
   C. type of registration of the vehicles
   D. police precincts in which the violations occurred

28. When pleading *Not Guilty* by mail to a parking violation, a motorist must select a hearing date.
The date the motorist may choose is any _____ days of the offense.

   A. weekday within 30
   B. weekday within 31 to 40
   C. day except Sunday within 60
   D. weekday within 60

29. If meters are to be installed in an area where four banks are located, the MOST suitable type to use would be _____ hour meters.

   A. 4   B. 1   C. 2   D. 3

30. Which one of these is NOT a part of the Transportation Administration?

   A. Department of Highways
   B. Department of Marine and Aviation
   C. Department of Traffic
   D. Bridge and Tunnel Authority

KEY (CORRECT ANSWERS)

1.	A	16.	C
2.	C	17.	A
3.	D	18.	B
4.	A	19.	C
5.	B	20.	B
6.	D	21.	C
7.	B	22.	A
8.	D	23.	C
9.	B	24.	C
10.	C	25.	C
11.	A	26.	D
12.	B	27.	D
13.	D	28.	B
14.	B	29.	A
15.	A	30.	D

TEST 3

DIRECTIONS: Each question or incomplete statement is followed by several suggested answers or completions. Select the one that BEST answers the question or completes the statement. *PRINT THE LETTER OF THE CORRECT ANSWER IN THE SPACE AT THE RIGHT.*

Questions 1-4.

DIRECTIONS: Questions 1 through 4 are to be answered ONLY according to the information given in the paragraph below.

    Abandoned cars — with tires gone, chrome stripped away, and windows smashed — have become a common sight on the city's streets. In 2000, more than 72,000 were deposited at curbs by owners who never came back, an increase of 15,000 from the year before and more than 30 times the number abandoned a decade ago. In January 2001, the city Protection Administrator asked the State Legislature to pass a law requiring a buyer of a new automobile to deposit $100 and an owner of an automobile at the time the law takes effect to deposit $50 with the State Department of Motor Vehicles. In return, they would be given a certificate of deposit that would be passed to each succeeding owner. The final owner would get the deposit money back if he could present proof that he has disposed of his car in an environmentally acceptable manner. The Legislature has given no indication that it planned to rush ahead on the matter.

1. The number of cars abandoned in city streets in 1999 was MOST NEARLY

    A. 2,500   B. 12,000   C. 27,500   D. 57,000

2. The proposed law would require a person who owned a car bought before the law was passed to deposit

    A. $100 with the State Department of Motor Vehicles
    B. $50 with the Environmental Protection Administration
    C. $100 with the State Legislature
    D. $50 with the State Department of Motor Vehicles

3. The proposed law would require the State to return the deposit money ONLY when the

    A. original owner of the car shows proof that he sold it
    B. last owner of the car shows proof that he got rid of the car in a satisfactory way
    C. owner of a car shows proof that he has transferred the certificate of deposit to the next owner
    D. last owner of a car returns the certificate of deposit

4. The MAIN idea or theme of the above article is that

    A. a proposed new law would make it necessary for car owners in the State to pay additional taxes
    B. the State Legislature is against a proposed law to require deposits from automobile owners to prevent them from abandoning their cars
    C. the city is trying to find a solution for the increasing number of cars abandoned on its streets

D. to pay for the removal of abandoned cars, the city's Environmental Protection Administrator has asked the State to fine automobile owners who abandon their vehicles

Questions 5-9.

DIRECTIONS: Questions 5 through 9 are to be answered ONLY according to the information given in the paragraph below.

Safety belts provide protection for the passengers of a vehicle by preventing them from crashing around inside if the vehicle is involved in a collision. They operate on the principle similar to that used in the packaging of fragile items. You become a part of the vehicle package, and you are kept from being tossed about inside if the vehicle is suddenly decelerated. Many injury-causing collisions at low speeds, for example at city intersections, could have been injury-free if the occupants had fastened their safety belts. There is a double advantage to the driver in that it not only protects him from harm, but prevents him from being yanked away from the wheel, thereby permitting him to maintain control of the car. Since without seat belts the risk of injury is about 50% greater, and the risk of death is about 30% greater, the New York State Vehicle and Traffic Law provides that a motor vehicle manufactured or assembled after June 30, 1964 and designated as a 1965 or later model should have two safety belts for the front seat. It also provides that a motor vehicle manufactured after June 30, 1966 and designated as a 1967 or later model should have at least one safety belt for the rear seat for each passenger for which the rear seat of such vehicle was designed.

5. The principle on which seat belts work is that 5.____

   A. a car and its driver and passengers are fragile
   B. a person fastened to the car will not be thrown around when the car slows down suddenly
   C. the driver and passengers of a car that is suddenly decelerated will be thrown forward
   D. the driver and passengers of an automobile should be packaged the way fragile items are packaged

6. We can assume from the above passage that safety belts should be worn at all times because you can NEVER tell when 6.____

   A. a car will be forced to turn off onto another road
   B. it will be necessary to shift into low gear to go up a hill
   C. you will have to speed up to pass another car
   D. a car may have to come to a sudden stop

7. Besides preventing injury, an additional benefit from the use of safety belts is that 7.____

   A. collisions are fewer
   B. damage to the car is kept down
   C. the car can be kept under control
   D. the number of accidents at city intersections is reduced

8. The risk of death in car accidents for people who don't use safety belts is 8.____

   A. 30% greater than the risk of injury
   B. 30% greater than for those who do use them

C. 50% less than the risk of injury
D. 50% greater than for those who use them

9. In the State, the number and location of safety belts required by law in a 1966 model car is two safety belts in the front seat

    A. only
    B. and one safety belt in the back seat
    C. and one safety belt for each person sitting in the back seat
    D. and three safety belts in the back seat of a 5-passenger car

10. Of the following, the MOST important reason for a supervisor to prepare good written reports is that

    A. a supervisor is rated on the quality of his reports
    B. decisions are often made on the basis of the reports
    C. such reports take less time for superiors to review
    D. such reports demonstrate efficiency of department operations

11. Of the following, the BEST test of a good report is whether it

    A. provides the information needed
    B. shows the good sense of the writer
    C. is prepared according to a proper format
    D. is grammatical and neat

12. When a supervisor writes a report, he can BEST show that he has an understanding of the subject of the report by

    A. including necessary facts and omitting non-essential details
    B. using statistical data
    C. giving his conclusions but not the data on which they are based
    D. using a technical vocabulary

13. Suppose you and another supervisor on the same level are assigned to work together on a report. You disagree strongly with one of the recommendations the other supervisor wants to include in the report but you cannot change his views.
    Of the following, it would be BEST that

    A. you refuse to accept responsibility for the report
    B. you ask that someone else be assigned to this project to replace you
    C. each of you state his own ideas about this recommendation in the report
    D. you give in to the other supervisor's opinion for the sake of harmony

14. Standardized forms are often provided for submitting reports.
    Of the following, the MOST important advantage of using standardized forms for reports is that

    A. they take less time to prepare than individually written reports
    B. the person making the report can omit information he considers unimportant
    C. the responsibility for preparing these reports can be turned over to subordinates
    D. necessary information is less likely to be omitte

15. A report which may BEST be classed as a periodic report is one which 15.____

    A. requires the same type of information at regular intervals
    B. contains detailed information which is to be retained in permanent records
    C. is prepared whenever a special situation occurs
    D. lists information in graphic form

16. When you drive so that you look ahead to possible mistakes by other drivers and prepare to take preventive action to make up for their mistakes, you are driving 16.____

    A. offensively   B. aggressively
    C. defensively   D. recklessly

17. The BEST reason for turning off the ignition of a motor vehicle when the gas tank is being filled is that, if this is not done, 17.____

    A. the carburetor may be damaged by the introduction of cold gasoline
    B. the fumes from the exhaust may overcome the person filling the tank
    C. an air block may develop in the vacuum feed line
    D. a spark from the electrical system may make the fumes of gasoline catch fire

18. If your car pulls to one side and you are not braking, it is probably a sign of 18.____

    A. worn-out shock absorbers
    B. worn rear tires
    C. unevenly distributed weight in the car
    D. worn or improperly adjusted steering mechanism

19. Almost 40 percent of the motor vehicle accidents in the state are rear end collisions. The use of proper following distances can prevent many of these accidents. The RECOMMENDED following distances (space between your car and the car in front) is 19.____

    A. one foot for each mile per hour of speed of your car
    B. two car lengths (about 40 feet) when traveling 30 miles per hour
    C. one car length (about 20 feet) for each ten miles per hour of speed of your car
    D. 60 feet at 60 miles per hour

20. The basic rule of driving conduct at an intersection is the rule of right-of-way. According to this rule, 20.____

    A. vehicles entering a traffic circle have right-of-way over those already in it
    B. pedestrians in crosswalks have right-of-way only if the traffic signal is in their favor
    C. at an intersection with no traffic control device, the car on your right has the privilege of going first
    D. a car turning left has the right-of-way over a vehicle going straight ahead

21. When you are being passed by another car, you should 21.____

    A. slow down and stay to your left
    B. slow down and stay to your right
    C. keep your normal speed so as not to confuse the driver of the other car
    D. keep your normal speed but move to the right

22. The flashing red signal on a traffic light has basically the SAME meaning for motorists as 22.____
    a

    A. steady yellow signal on a traffic light
    B. yield sign
    C. stop sign
    D. red arrow signal on a traffic light

23. When driving, after you pass a car, you should immediately signal your return to the right 23.____
    lane and then swing back into this lane when

    A. you can see the car's front bumper in your rearview mirror
    B. the car you are passing has signaled that it is safe to return to the right lane
    C. the car you are passing is out of sight
    D. you can see pavement in front of the car just passed as you look quickly over your shoulder

24. The type of street marking that cannot be crossed by traffic going in either direction 24.____
    except for a left turn into or out of a driveway or alley is a

    A. single solid white line
    B. double broken white line with white edges
    C. single solid yellow line with a parallel broken white line
    D. double solid yellow line

25. A state traffic sign with a down-pointed triangle would MOST likely warn the driver to 25.____

    A. yield   B. detour
    C. stop   D. keep right except to pass

KEY (CORRECT ANSWERS)

1. A		11. A	
2. D		12. A	
3. B		13. C	
4. C		14. D	
5. B		15. A	
6. D		16. C	
7. C		17. D	
8. B		18. D	
9. A		19. C	
10. B		20. C	

21. B
22. C
23. A
24. D
25. A

EXAMINATION SECTION
TEST 1

DIRECTIONS: Each question or incomplete statement is followed by several suggested answers or completions. Select the one that BEST answers the question or completes the statement. *PRINT THE LETTER OF THE CORRECT ANSWER IN THE SPACE AT THE RIGHT.*

1. When a vehicle is so large that it must use two metered parking spaces, it should be parked

   A. with its front end alongside the forward meter and a coin deposited only in the forward meter
   B. with its front end alongside the forward meter and coins deposited in the meters for each, of the spaces filled by the vehicle
   C. with its tail end alongside the rear meter and a coin deposited in the meter closest to the rear of the vehicle
   D. in the approximate middle of the two spaces and a coin deposited in either of the meters alongside the vehicle

   1.____

2. A senior enforcement agent finds the following cars parked at expired meters at a time when meter regulations are in effect:
   I. A vehicle with FC plates
   II. A vehicle with a Patrolman's Benevolent Association card on the sun visor
   III. An unmarked vehicle displaying a blue metal shield identifying it as a City Police Department car

   Which of the above vehicles should be given summonses?

   A. I, but not II and III
   B. II, but not I and III
   C. I and II, but not III
   D. II and III, but not I

   2.____

3. An enforcement agent mistakenly issues a summons to an unoccupied automobile parked at a meter at a time when parking is not restricted. The agent realizes his error before the driver of the automobile returns.
   In this situation, the agent should

   A. destroy the summons but make a note of the circumstnces under which it was issued on the back of the agency copy
   B. leave a note on the automobile to the motorist telling him to disregard the summons since it was issued in error
   C. allow the motorist to receive the summons since the error can be corrected later
   D. return the summons to the district commander with a written memo describing the circumstances under which it was issued

   3.____

4. Following are three practices a senior enforcement agent observes while on patrol:
   I. A person reserving a parking space in front of a fruit store by placing a crate in the roadway
   II. A motorcycle five feet long parked at an angle to the curb with one wheel touching the curb
   III. A food vendor parked at a metered parking space selling sodas and ice cream to passing pedestrians

   4.____

Which one of the following correctly classifies the above practices into those which are LAWFUL and those which are NOT?

    A. I is lawful, but II and III are not
    B. II is lawful, but I and III are not
    C. II and III are lawful, but I is not
    D. I, II and III are not lawful

5. The MAIN purpose of instructing department enforcement personnel to disregard fraternal, labor, social, religious, and political identifications on vehicles is to

    A. provide for impartial enforcement of regulations
    B. simplify the work of Parking Enforcement Agents
    C. make sure that no one group gets more summonses than any other group
    D. increase the number of summonses issued

6. During the absence of the district commander, one of the senior enforcement agents from that district may be assigned to perform the duties of the district commander. If no one has been specifically named to take over this job, the senior who takes over for the district commander is the one

    A. with the most seniority
    B. who reports to work first
    C. scheduled for a regular day off
    D. who has not previously substituted for the district commander

7. While you are checking an area, a motorist in a private car complains to you that an agent issued a summons to him for double parking but that a passenger car parked right behind him did not get a summons.
The BEST action for you to take is to tell him

    A. to give you all the information and you will investigate the matter
    B. to call the main office
    C. that it was probably just an oversight and you will speak to the agent
    D. that whether or not the other driver got a summons is not his business

8. Special Vehicle Identification permits issued to handicapped drivers permit the holders to park

    A. in areas regulated by "No Parking" signs
    B. in areas regulated by "No Stopping" signs
    C. at fire hydrants
    D. at taxi stands

9. The one of the following items which does NOT have to be entered on an enforcement agent's field patrol sheet is the

    A. report of an abandoned car which does not have a Sanitation Department sticker
    B. completion of Univac (computer) cards to report missing, defective or vandalized meters
    C. listing of the locations of the agent's personal and meal breaks
    D. notation that the agent observed collectors from a Finance Department truck collecting money from parking meters

10. Assume that standing is prohibited in a certain area. According to the traffic regulations, the driver of a passenger vehicle in that area would be permitted to

    A. stand in front of a private driveway
    B. stop to discharge passengers
    C. park temporarily in order to unload merchandise
    D. stand for a period of no more than ten minutes provided he remains in the car

11. According to the traffic regulations, the MINIMUM period of time a vehicle may be parked before it is considered to be parked for the principal purpose of storing the vehicle is

    A. 12 hours   B. 24 hours   C. 36 hours   D. 48 hours

12. An enforcement agent finds each of the following three vehicles parked on a street with no posted parking restrictions:
    I. A van with commercial plates which has been parked in front of a store for six hours
    II. A car parked at the curb while the owner is changing a flat tire
    III. A car parked in front of a private home while the owner is washing the car

    According to the traffic regulations, *which one* of the following CORRECTLY classifies the above vehicles into those which should receive summonses and those which should not?

    A. I and II should receive summonses, but III should not
    B. II and III should receive summonses, but I should not
    C. I and III should receive summonses, but II should not
    D. I, II, and III should receive summonses

13. A senior enforcement agent should inspect the uniform and equipment of each member of his squad at least once a

    A. day   B. week   C. pay-period   D. month

14. When a senior enforcement agent cannot locate the parking enforcement agent assigned to a patrol area, she notes this fact and the time on her field patrol sheet. According to bureau procedures the FIRST action the senior should take when she sees the missing agent is to

    A. order the agent to report to the district commander
    B. ask the agent for an explanation of the absence
    C. check the agent's field patrol sheet to see if there was a reason for the absence
    D. submit a report on the incident to the district commander

15. In addition to their daily enforcement duties, senior enforcement agents are generally required to

    A. accompany agents to a hospital when agents are injured or assaulted
    B. make out probationary reports on clerical personnel
    C. deliver completed summonses to the parking violations bureau
    D. deliver notices of special assignments to agents who are off duty

16. An enforcement agent should be instructed to issue a summons to a car

    A. that forms part of a funeral procession, double-parked in front of a funeral parlor
    B. with DPL plates parked in a "No Standing" zone
    C. with MD plates parked for two hours in front of a hospital
    D. that displays an SVI card parked in a "No Parking" zone

17. An enforcement agent observes the driver of a passenger vehicle discharging passengers at a bus stop.
    Of the following, the MOST appropriate action for the agent to take is to

    A. continue on patrol
    B. issue a summons
    C. warn the driver that what he is doing is illegal
    D. politely ask the driver to move

18. The *one* of the following who usually assigns enforcement agents to their daily patrol areas and rotates the agents from one patrol area to another is the

    A. senior enforcement agent
    B. district commander
    C. regional commander
    D. chief of the traffic control bureau

19. An enforcement agent on patrol discovers a traffic signal out of order.
    The FIRST of the following actions the agent should take is to

    A. regulate traffic at the intersection himself until repair service arrives
    B. inform the Police Department of the problem
    C. notify Control 800 on his portable radio
    D. note the problem on the back of his field patrol sheet

20. Following are three statements concerning the uniforms and personal appearance of enforcement agents:
    I. Dangling earrings and numerous rings are not to be worn on duty.
    II. Uniforms may be worn to and from work.
    III. A neat beard and trimmed mustache may be worn.
    Which of the following classifies the above statements into those which are CORRECT and those which are NOT?

    A. I is correct, but II and III are not
    B. II is correct, but I and III are not
    C. II and III are correct, but I is not
    D. I and III are correct, but II is not

21. Of the following, a senior enforcement agent is responsible for

    A. setting-up the weekly roll call
    B. taking portable radios for necessary repairs
    C. approving transfer requests
    D. investigating reports of lost summonses

22. Assume that a private vehicle has stopped at an unmarked crosswalk to permit a pedestrian to cross the roadway. According to the traffic regulations concerning passing, the driver of another private vehicle approaching from the rear may

   A. pass the stopped vehicle
   B. not pass the stopped vehicle
   C. pass the stopped vehicle only if weather conditions make it possible to do so safely
   D. not pass the stopped vehicle unless he does so from the left

23. A senior enforcement agent notices that some of the agents in his squad have written their rank and signature in ink on several books of summonses before they go out into the field.
   According to traffic control bureau policy, this practice is

   A. *advisable,* PRIMARILY because it saves the agents time in the field
   B. *advisable,* PRIMARILY because those summonses cannot be taken and used by other agents
   C. *inadvisable,* PRIMARILY because an agent may resign or be transferred, leaving the district office with several pre-signed summonses
   D. *inadvisable,* PRIMARILY because it wastes time in the district office

24. A senior enforcement agent notices that the uniform of one of the agents under his supervision is in such poor condition that the senior believes it should be replaced. According to traffic control bureau procedures, the NEXT step the senior should take is to

   A. order the agent to purchase a new uniform
   B. check to see that the agent purchases a new uniform within 10 days
   C. make a note that the agent needs a new uniform and report this fact to the district commander at the next uniform inspection
   D. ask the district commander to inspect the agent's uniform as soon as possible

25. A senior enforcement agent on patrol hears the following messages exchanged between an enforcement agent and the radio dispatcher:
   ENFORCEMENT AGENT: 10-15, New York Plate IDA MARY PETER 1 - 2 - 3 - 4, K
   DISPATCHER: 10-4, 10-6, K
   This is followed by :
   DISPATCHER: New York Plate IDA MARY PETER 1-2-3-4, 10-17, K
   ENFORCEMENT AGENT: 10-4, K
   Which one of the following BEST describes this exchange of messages?

   A. The agent is calling for a tow truck for a vehicle with New York license plate number IMP 1234, and the Dispatcher verifies that a tow truck is on the way
   B. The agent is requesting information on a vehicle that may be stolen and the Dispatcher responds that the vehicle is not listed as stolen
   C. The agent is requesting information on a vehicle that may be stolen and the Dispatcher responds that the vehicle is listed as stolen
   D. The agent is reporting an accident involving a vehicle with New York license plate IMP 1234, and the Dispatcher verifies that the message has been received

26. Which one of the following is the PROPER way for an agent to correct a summons on which the agent entered an incorrect license plate number?

    A. Draw a line through the incorrect number and write the correction immediately above it
    B. Issue a new, correct summons and submit the original summons with a memo reporting the mistake to the district commander
    C. Discard the summons and the stub and renumber the next summons
    D. Erase the mistake, enter the correct information, initial the correction, and complete the summons

27. *When* should luminous safety vests and white glbves be worn by traffic control agents who are directing traffic? Luminous safety vests

    A. should be worn only during hours of darkness, and white gloves as weather conditions dictate
    B. should be worn at all times, and white gloves only during hours of daylight
    C. should be worn only during hours of darkness, and white gloves at all times
    D. and white gloves should be worn at all times

28. According to traffic control bureau procedures, *how frequently* should performance evaluation reports on probationary enforcement agents be prepared by senior enforcement agents?

    A. Every sixty days during the first year of employment
    B. Once a month during the first six months of employment
    C. Twice a month during the first year of employment
    D. Every week during the first six months of employment

29. Following are three statements concerning the use of time and leave in the traffic control bureau:
    I. An employee with more than twelve latenesses in any vacation year shall be charged double time for the latenesses.
    II. Sick leave is accrued at, the rate of 1 1/2 days a month.
    III. A request tp take time off for personal business must be submitted at least five days in advance.

    Which one of the following correctly classifies the above statements into those which are CORRECT and those which are NOT?

    A. I and II are correct, but III is not
    B. II and III are correct, but I is not
    C. II is correct, but I and III are not
    D. III is correct, but I and II are not

30. Traffic signs on certain streets indicate that stopping, standing or parking regulations do NOT apply on Sundays. These regulations are also suspended on certain holidays.
    Which of the following is NOT one of these "Sunday" holidays?

    A. Election Day   B. Labor Day
    C. Independence Day   D. Memorial Day

31. When the traffic commissioner declares a state of snow emergency, NO person may operate a

    A. commercial vehicle on any street unless the vehicle is equipped with snow tires or chains
    B. vehicle in Manhattan on any cross street between 59th Street and the Battery unless the vehicle is equipped with snow tires or chains
    C. vehicle on the Brooklyn-Queens Expressway unless the vehicle is equipped with snow tires or chains
    D. taxicab on any street in the city unless the vehicle is equipped with chains

32. A traffic control agent should NOT issue a summons when a vehicle makes an illegal left turn if the vehicle is

    A. a car with MD license plates
    B. a Sanitation Department sweeper engaged in cleaning the street
    C. an official State government vehicle
    D. a limousine with diplomatic license plates

33. An enforcement agent who has been assaulted and injured calls 911 for police assistance. When the police arrive, it would be INCORRECT for the agent to

    A. let the police know he is injured and needs immediate medical attention
    B. give both his office and home address to the police
    C. notify the district office of his location and tell the office that the police have been summoned
    D. take down the name, shield number and precinct of each police officer who participates in the incident

34. The duties of a senior parking enforcement agent include all of the following EXCEPT

    A. distributing carfare to agents
    B. filing charges against agents
    C. assisting in the training of newly assigned agents
    D. sending memos directly to the assistant director of the traffic control bureau

35. A senior parking enforcement agent should advise a traffic control agent that, while on duty at an intersection, it is generally proper to do all of the following EXCEPT

    A. give brief directions to motorists stopped for a light
    B. leave the intersection to report a fire by pulling a fire alarm box
    C. monitor all calls on his radio to learn of conditions which might cause delays in his area
    D. leave the intersection for a rest break between 7:00 a.m. and 9:00 a.m.

36. The one of the following duties which is NOT normally assigned to a senior parking enforcement agent is

    A. going on car patrol
    B. approving vacation requests
    C. observing the on-the-job performance of traffic control agents
    D. dropping off and picking up parking enforcement agents at distant field assignments

37. A senior parking enforcement agent has a tire "blowout" while driving an official department motor vehicle.
All of the following are generally correct actions to take in this situation EXCEPT

   A. steering straight ahead
   B. keeping a firm grip on the steering wheel
   C. braking quickly to stop the car
   D. releasing the gas pedal

38. While driving a department motor vehicle along the highway, you feel the car pull to the right. This is LEAST likely to be a sign of possible trouble with the

   A. steering mechanism B. wheel alignment
   C. transmission   D. tires

39. It has been suggested that a driver should expect other drivers to do the wrong thing and be ready with a plan of action to counter the other driver's errors. Following this practice can BEST be described as

   A. *advisable,* CHIEFLY because it develops a driver's skill in handling his vehicle
   B. *advisable,* CHIEFLY because it helps to avoid accidents
   C. *inadvisable,* CHIEFLY because most other drivers follow the rules of the road
   D. *inadvisable,* CHIEFLY because it takes the driver's attention away from immediate conditions

40. A senior parking enforcement agent is driving an official department motor vehicle on patrol. She notices that the red emergency light is on, indicating that the engine is overheated. She sees steam coming out from under the engine hood.
Of the following, the MOST appropriate action for the senior to take in this situation is to

   A. stop the car, open the engine hood, get a pail of cold water, and pour it over the engine
   B. stop the car, open the engine hood, remove the radiator cap, and relieve the steam pressure in the radiator
   C. stop the car, open the engine hood, wait until the car cools down, then drive it to the nearest service station
   D. continue driving the car, but take it ti the repair shops instead of continuing on patrol

KEY (CORRECT ANSWERS)

1. A	11. B	21. B	31. C
2. C	12. C	22. B	32. B
3. D	13. A	23. C	33. B
4. B	14. C	24. D	34. D
5. A	15. A	25. B	35. D
6. A	16. B	26. B	36. B
7. A	17. A	27. D	37. C
8. A	18. B	28. B	38. C
9. D	19. C	29. D	39. B
10. B	20. A	30. A	40. C

TEST 2

DIRECTIONS: Each question or incomplete statement is followed by several suggested answers or completions. Select the one that BEST answers the question or completes the statement. *PRINT THE LETTER OF THE CORRECT ANSWER IN THE SPACE AT THE RIGHT.*

1. Department procedures permit operation of a department motor vehicle even when there is   1.____

    A. white exhaust vapor
    B. no transmission oil
    C. overheating
    D. low oil pressure

2. Following are three statements concerning safe following distances in highway driving: 2.____
    I. When traveling at 40 miles per hour on dry pavement, allow about 80 feet between your car and the car in front of you
    II. When driving at night at any speed, you will be able to stop within the distance lighted by your car's headlights
    III. When traveling at 30 miles per hour on wet pavement, allow about 60 feet of space between your car and the car in front of you

    Which one of the following *correctly* classifies the above statements into those which are CORRECT and those which are NOT?

    A. I is correct, but II and III are not
    B. II is correct, but I and III are not
    C. I and II are correct, but III is not
    D. I and III are correct, but II is not

3. Following are three statements concerning driving practices at intersections: 3.____
    I. When making a right turn, place your vehicle so as to block any vehicle that might try to squeeze between you and the curb
    II. When making a left turn, have your wheels turned while waiting for traffic to clear
    III. When driving through an intersection, have you foot off the accelerator and on the brake pedal as you approach the intersection

    Which one of the following *correctly* classifies the above statements into those that are PROPER and those that are NOT?

    A. I and II are proper, but III is not
    B. I and III are proper, but II is not
    C. II and III are proper, but I is not
    D. I, II and III are proper

4. Following are three statements concerning pedestrians in the city: 4.____
    I. Pedestrians are permitted to stand in the road to sell merchandise to passing motorists
    II. Pedestrians under 14 years of age typically have quick reaction time, good judgment, and are seldom involved in accidents
    III. Pedestrians may not always have the legal right of way but cars must always yield the right of way to a pedestrian

    Which one of the following *correctly* classifies the above statements into those which are CORRECT and those which are NOT?

    A. I and II are correct, but III is not
    B. II and III are correct, but I is not
    C. II is correct, but I and III are not
    D. III is correct, but I and II are not

2 (#2)

QUESTIONS 5 and 6.

Questions 5 and 6 are based on the information given on the report forms pictured below and on the following page.

Chart I and Chart II are parts of the Field Patrol Sheets of two Parking Enforcement Agents. They show the numbers of violations issued on a particular day. Chart III is the Tally Sheet for that day prepared by the Senior Parking Enforcement Agent from the Field Patrol Sheets of the entire squad.

Chart I

Area or Post	TYPE OF VIOLATION											
	Mtrs	B/S	D/P	Hyd	N/S	N/Sp	Taxi	Curb	N/P	Alt	Other	Total
19	2	3	2	2	3	3	0	1	1	5	1	23
21	4	0	2	0	1	2	2	0	5	9	1	26
Totals	6	3	4	2	4	5	2	1	6	14	2	49

Date: 2/4/   Badge: 100   Signature: PEA Browne

TCB-61   Checked by _____ Date _____

Chart II

Area or Post	TYPE OF VIOLATION											
	Mtrs	B/S	D/P	Hyd	N/S	N/Sp	Taxi	Curb	N/P	Alt	Other	Total
31	8	2	0	0	3	2	2	0	4	5	0	26
33	7	0	1	2	3	1	2	0	6	3	0	25
Totals	15	2	1	2	6	3	4	0	10	8	0	51

Date: 2/4/   Badge: 101   Signature: PEA Grey

TCB-61   Checked by _____ Date _____

Chart III

Name	Mtrs Ptld	Mtrs	Bus Stop	Dble Park	Hyd	No Stand	No Stop	Taxi Stand	Curb	No Park	Alt Park	Other	Total
					TRAFFIC CONTROL BUREAU SENIORS TALLY SHEET							Enf. 23A	
Green		18	2	3	1	6	0	0	0	4	10	1	45
Browne		6	3	4	2	4	5	2	1	6	14	2	49
White		12	0	0	0	2	1	1	0	8	8	1	33
Black		20	5	2	3	8	7	5	1	5	4	0	60
Grey		15	2	1	2	9	3	4	0	10	8	0	51
Redding		17	0	1	3	7	5	3	0	8	6	0	50
TOTAL		88	12	11	11	36	21	15	2	41	50	4	288

5. The Senior Parking Enforcement Agent who prepared Chart III made an error in transferring the violation totals from the Field Patrol Sheets to the Seniors Tally Sheet. Which one of the following properly describes the Tally Sheet entry if this error were corrected?

    A. Parking Enforcement Agent Browne's overall total of summonses issued would be 50
    B. Parking Enforcement Agent Browne's total of summonses issued for Double-Parking violations would be 3
    C. Parking Enforcement Agent Grey's total number of summonses issued for meter violations would be 6
    D. Parking Enforcement Agent Grey's total number of summonses issued for No Standing violations would be 6

6. The parking enforcement agent who issued the MOST summonses for bus stop and taxi stand violations is

    A. Black   B. Redding   C. White   D. Browne

7. A senior parking enforcement agent is shown a copy of an "Employee's Notice of Injury" form from an Agent who has been injured while on duty. Following is part of that report:

    5. Exact location where accident happened. One-half block West of the Northwest corner of Seventh Avenue and 34th Street. (in front of 225 West 34th Street.)
    6. How did accident happen? (describe fully) I slipped in the street because I didn't look where I was going.
    7. Nature and extent of injury. Broken foot
    8. Did you inform your superior of this accident? Yes   Date? Thursday

Which of the following lists ALL of the item numbers which the senior should point out to the agent as missing necessary information?

A. 5 and 6
B. 5, 6 and 7
C. 5, 6 and 8
D. 6, 7 and 8

8. For which of the following is the information recorded on the parking enforcement agent's field patrol sheets LEAST likely to be useful to a Senior Parking Enforcement Agent?

A. Gathering evidence for use in a disciplinary action against an agent
B. Determining whether agents have been enforcing regulations
C. Learning which agents have the most problems dealing with the public
D. Investigating a complaint that an agent has been absent from his post for several hours

8.____

9. Just as a parking enforcement agent has put a summons on an illegally parked car, the driver of the car comes out of a luncheonette and begins calling her names.
Of the following, the FIRST action the agent should take in this situation is to

A. ask the driver to apologize
B. call for police assistance
C. call the supervisor for assistance
D. walk away and say nothing

9.____

10. A senior parking enforcement agent is assigned to instruct the staff of a district office on the use of a new one-page form which will be put into use next month.
Of the following, the BEST way to teach the staff about this new form is to

A. call a staff meeting to explain the use of the new form and find out if the agents have any questions about its use
B. post the new form and the instructions for completing it on a bulletin board in the District Office
C. explain the use of the new form at morning roll call just before the agents go into the field
D. issue a written instruction booklet to each staff member

10.____

11. A person asks a traffic control agent for the address of a neighborhood restaurant and directions to it.
If the agent is unfamiliar with the restaurant, it would generally be BEST for him to tell the person

A. that he is sorry, but he has not heard of the restaurant and is unable to direct him
B. to look up the restaurant's address in a telephone book and come back to the agent for exact directions
C. to find a policeman who should be able to direct him
D. to look up the restaurant in a telephone book and phone them for directions

11.____

12. A senior parking enforcement agent on patrol observes an agent and a motorist shouting loudly and angrily at each other. It appears that a fight might start at any moment. Of the following, it would be MOST appropriate for the senior to

    A. continue on patrol and ask the agent about the incident at the end of the tour
    B. observe the incident from a distance and allow the agent to handle this situation alone
    C. tell the agent that he will try to handle the situation himself
    D. calm the motorist by scolding the agent in front of the motorist

13. An enforcement agent reports that one of the merchants in his patrol area with whom he is quite friendly has offered him a gift as a token of thanks for keeping people from misusing the parking spaces in front of his store. The agent explains that he would probably offend the merchant by rejecting the merchandise offered.
    The senior should advise this agent

    A. *not to accept* the gift, CHIEFLY because other agents do not receive such gifts
    B. *not to accept* the gift, CHIEFLY because acceptance would violate the department code of conduct
    C. *to accept* the gift, CHIEFLY because the Department prides itself on maintaining a good relationship with neighborhood merchants
    D. *to accept* the gift, CHIEFLY because a gift is a personal matter between two friends and has nothing to do with the job

14. An enforcement agent whose performance has been generally good tells his senior that he would like to discuss some personal problems that have been interfering with his work. In this situation, it would generally be MOST appropriate for the senior to

    A. tell the agent he has not noticed any change in his work lately and that his problems cannot be too serious
    B. listen while the agent discusses his problems, but refer him for professional counseling if his problems seem serious
    C. tell the agent that it is his responsibility to solve his own personal problems
    D. ask one of the agent's close friends on the job to have a talk with him and find out the nature of the problem

15. An enforcement agent has just completed a summons for a meter violation when the driver approaches. The driver is annoyed and demands that the summons be destroyed. Of the following, *which* is the MOST appropriate response for the agent to make?

    A. "I'm extremely sorry, sir, but I'm only doing my job."
    B. "I'm supposed to enforce the regulations strictly and without exception."
    C. "Leave me alone, mister, we're not allowed to tear up tickets."
    D. "Don't you know enough to put a dime in the meter, like everyone else parked on this block?"

16. A senior enforcement agent on foot patrol is checking summonses on parked cars. He finds a summons on which the "scheduled fine" box is not filled in. The agent who issued the summons has already left the area.
    In this situation, it would be MOST appropriate for the senior to

    A. leave the summons as it is, since the motorist can find out the amount of the fine himself
    B. find the agent and tell him to return to the car, fill in the missing information, and make a notation of the error in the district office at the end of the tour
    C. fill in the correct amount of fine on the summons and make a note on the field patrol sheet to mention the error to the agent at the end of the tour
    D. have the agent write a memorandum describing the error

17. Praise by a supervisor can be an important element in motivating subordinates. Following are three statements concerning a supervisor's praise of subordinates:
    I. In order to be effective, praise must be lavish and constantly restated.
    II. Praise should be given in a manner which meets the needs of the individual subordinate.
    III. The subordinate whose work is praised should believe that the praise is earned.

    Which of the following correctly classifies the above statements into those that are CORRECT and those that are NOT?

    A. I is correct, but II and III are not
    B. II and III are correct, but I is not
    C. III is correct, but I and II are not
    D. I and II are correct, but III is not

18. Assume that you are a senior enforcement agent and that several of the recently appointed agents on your squad have not been adequately enforcing alternate side of the street parking regulations.
    Of the following, the MOST appropriate way for you to correct this situation is to

    A. begin disciplinary proceedings against the individuals involved
    B. call a brief meeting of your squad to review the regulations and emphasize the need for strict enforcement
    C. spend more of your own patrol time issuing summonses for violations of alternate side of the street parking regulations
    D. reprimand the entire squad during Roll Call for not enforcing alternate side of the street regulations

19. A senior enforcement agent notices that although there have been several defective meters in a recently appointed agent's patrol area, the agent has not turned in any of the Univac cards used to report broken parking meters.
    Of the following, it would be MOST appropriate for the senior to assume that the

    A. district office has run out of these cards
    B. agent has spent too much time loafing to locate any broken meters
    C. agent should be disciplined for not turning in these cards
    D. agent may need more training in detecting broken meters and filling out the Univac cards

20. A senior enforcement agent, upon arriving in the district office for the 7:30AM-3:30PM tour, finds that the agent assigned to cover a priority patrol area has called in sick.
Of the following, it would generally be MOST appropriate for the senior to

    A. notify the district commander that there is no coverage for the priority patrol area
    B. call in an agent who is scheduled for a regular day off to cover the priority patrol area
    C. shift the patrol assignment of another agent to the priority patrol area
    D. cover the priority area personally while out on patrol

21. Following are three statements concerning various ways of giving orders to enforcement agents:
    I. An implied order or suggestion is usually appropriate for the inexperienced agent.
    II. A polite request is less likely to upset a sensitive agent than a direct order.
    III. A direct order is usually appropriate in an emergency situation.

    Which of the following correctly classifies the above statements into those that are CORRECT and those that are NOT?

    A. I is correct, but II and III are not
    B. II and III are correct, but I is not
    C. III is correct, but I and II are not
    D. I and II are correct, but III is not

22. A senior enforcement agent on patrol observes two agents entering a bar and ordering beer when they should be on patrol.
Of the following, the *correct* procedure for the senior to follow is to

    A. note how long they remain in the bar, say nothing to them at the time, but speak to the agents when they return to the district office
    B. make no note of the incident and quietly tell the agents to leave the bar and continue their patrol duties
    C. call the District Commander immediately to report the incident, and tell the agents to proceed directly to the district office
    D. tell the agents to return to duty, enter the incident on his field patrol sheet and on theirs, and submit a memo to the District Commander at the end of the tour

23. A senior enforcement agent feels that he is about to lose his temper while reprimanding a subordinate.
Of the following, the BEST action for the senior to take is to

    A. postpone the reprimand for a short time until his self-control is assured
    B. continue the reprimand because a loss of temper by the senior will show the subordinate the seriousness of the error he made
    C. continue the reprimand because failure to do so will show that the senior does not have complete self-control
    D. postpone the reprimand until the subordinate is capable of understanding the reason for the supervisor's loss of temper

24. Daily inspections by senior enforcement agents of their subordinates' uniforms are useful *chiefly* because

    A. they show the department that the seniors are performing their duties
    B. subordinates learn to expect the inspections and follow the rules automatically
    C. they help to insure the proper appearance of the agents before the public
    D. subordinates appreciate the attention they receive form their superiors

25. While in the field, an enforcement agent asks a senior a question about how to request maternity leave from the Department of Traffic. The senior does not know the answer.
    Of the following, it would be BEST for the senior to tell the agent

    A. to wait until she is ready to leave before inquiring about maternity leave
    B. that he does not know the answer but will get the information for her as soon as possible
    C. to call the District Commander from the field
    D. to write to her union representative

26. Enforcement agent Jones tells a senior enforcement agent that agent Smith has been taking lunch breaks of up to two hours.
    Of the following, the FIRST thing for the senior to do in this situation is to

    A. tell agent Jones to stop gossiping about her fellow employees
    B. refer the matter to the District Commander for investigation
    C. take disciplinary action against agent Smith
    D. investigate the matter and get all the facts from both agents

27. During their probationary period, parking enforcement and traffic control agents are informed of deficiencies in their performance.
    This practice is

    A. *good,* chiefly because agents learn where they need to improve
    B. *good,* chiefly because agents can defend themselves against false charges
    C. *poor,* chiefly because agents may become easily discouraged
    D. *poor,* chiefly because any improvement in performance is likely to be temporary

28. Of the following, the MOST practical method of providing on-the-job training for newly assigned enforcement agents who have just completed the course at the training division is for the senior to

    A. assign each new agent to go out on patrol with a more experienced agent until the new agent learns the job
    B. have the new agents accompany the senior on patrol for about two weeks
    C. accompany the new agents on patrol for the first half of their tour each day, but let them patrol on their own for the last half
    D. give each agent his own patrol area to cover alone, thus letting him learn the job by doing it

29. A senior enforcement agent should generally give an *oral* order rather than a *written* order to subordinates when

    A. a precise record of the instructions given in the order is required
    B. the subordinates must refresh their memories from time to time to properly carry out the order

C. the order is a very complicated one
D. the order involves a routine activity which the subordinates have performed properly in the past

30. The one of the following which is NOT a valid principle for a supervisor to keep in mind when talking to a subordinate about his performance is:

    A. People frequently know when they deserve criticism
    B. Supervisors should be prepared to offer suggestions to subordinates about how to improve their work
    C. Good points should be discussed before bad points
    D. Magnifying a subordinate's faults will get him to improve faster

31. In many organizations information travels quickly through the "grapevine". Following are three statements concerning the "grapevine":
    I. Information an enforcement agent does not want to tell her supervisor may reach the supervisor through the grapevine.
    II. A supervisor can often do her job better by knowing the information that travels through the grapevine.
    III. A supervisor can depend on the grapevine as a way to get accurate information from the enforcement agents on her staff.

    Which one of the following correctly classifies the above statements into those which are generally CORRECT and those which are NOT?

    A. II is correct, but I and III are not
    B. III is correct, but I and II are not
    C. I and II are correct, but III is not
    D. I and III are correct, but II is not

32. The Traffic Control Bureau has received a letter of complaint from a member of the public about an enforcement agent. Preliminary investigation shows that the complaint appears to be unjustified and that the subordinate is completely innocent.
    Of the following, it would generally be MOST appropriate for the agent's supervisor to

    A. proceed no further since the complaint is unjustified
    B. transfer the subordinate to another patrol assignment to prevent possible contact with the same member of the public
    C. make no note of the complaint on a complaint record form because any entry in the files could harm the subordinate's career
    D. complete a thorough investigation of the matter and fill out a complaint record form

33. Following are three statements concerning supervision:
    I. A supervisor knows he is doing a good job if his subordinates depend upon him to make every decision
    II. A supervisor who delegates authority to his subordinates soon finds that his subordinates begin to resent him.
    III. Giving credit for good work is frequently an effective method of getting subordinates to work harder.

    Which one of the following correctly classifies the above statements into those that are CORRECT and those that are NOT?

    A. I and II are correct, but III is not
    B. II and III are correct, but I is not

C. II is correct, but I and III are not
D. III is correct, but I and II are not

34. Preparing supervisors to carry out their training responsibilities is the most effective training activity that can be carried on.
Applying this principle to senior enforcement agents would be

    A. *undesirable,* chiefly because adequate training is given to all enforcement agents at the training division
    B. *undesirable,* chiefly because training supervisors is costly and inefficient
    C. *desirable,* chiefly because training of subordinates by supervisors who are trained to teach is generaly helpful
    D. *desirable,* chiefly because it gives the seniors an added job function

35. Training senior enforcement agents to take over the job of the District Commander when the District Commander is absent is *generally*

    A. *desirable,* chiefly because it increases staff flexibility and the district's readiness to handle emergencies
    B. *desirable,* chiefly because it enables seniors to pass promotion examinations
    C. *undesirable,* chiefly because errors made by the seniors during such training cannot be corrected
    D. *undesirable,* chiefly because Department of Traffic regulations forbid seniors from performing the District Commander's job

36. Following are three statements concerning on-the-job training:
    I. On-the-job training is rarely used as a method of training employees.
    II. On-the-job training is often carried on with little or no planning.
    III. On-the-job training is often less expensive than other types of training.
    Which one of the following BEST classifies the above statements into those that are CORRECT and those that are NOT?

    A. I is correct, but II and III are not
    B. II is correct, but I and III are not
    C. I and II are correct, but III is not
    D. II and III are correct, but I is not

37. The one of the following that is the MOST appropriate action for a senior enforcement agent to take when criticizing a subordinate for carelessness in making out summonses is to

    A. make the subordinate feel ashamed of his work
    B. direct his criticism at specific mistakes made by the subordinate
    C. focus his comments on the subordinate's overall job performance
    D. tell the subordinate that his carelessness shows that he is unable to handle the job

38. Of the following, the LEAST appropriate action for a supervisor to take in preparing a disciplinary case against a subordinate is to

    A. keep careful records of each incident in which the subordinate has been guilty of misconduct or incompetency, even though immediate disciplinary action may not be necessary
    B. discuss with the employee each incident of misconduct as it occurs so the employee knows where he stands
    C. accept memoranda from any other employees who may have been witnesses to acts of misconduct
    D. keep the subordinate's personnel file confidential so that he is unaware of the evidence being gathered against him

39. Traffic control agents on duty at intersections should be instructed by their supervisors to do all of the following EXCEPT

    A. stand in the center of the intersection of two-way streets
    B. turn in the direction in which traffic is moving
    C. direct turning vehicles to complete their turns behind him
    D. move from place to place within an intersection of a one-way street, as traffic conditions change

40. The one of the following which is NOT an acceptable reason for taking disciplinary action against a subordinate guilty of serious violations of the rules is that

    A. the supervisor can "let off steam" against subordinates who break rules frequently
    B. a subordinate whose work continues to be unsatisfactory may be terminated
    C. a subordinate may be encouraged to improve his work
    D. an example is set for other employees

KEY (CORRECT ANSWERS)

1. A	11. B	21. B	31. C
2. A	12. C	22. D	32. D
3. B	13. B	23. A	33. D
4. D	14. B	24. C	34. C
5. D	15. B	25. B	35. A
6. A	16. C	26. D	36. D
7. D	17. B	27. A	37. B
8. C	18. B	28. A	38. D
9. D	19. D	29. D	39. C
10. A	20. C	30. D	40. A

SUPERVISION, ADMINISTRATION, MANAGEMENT AND ORGANIZATION
EXAMINATION SECTION
TEST 1

DIRECTIONS: Each question or incomplete statement is followed by several suggested answers or completions. Select the one that BEST answers the question or completes the statement. *PRINT THE LETTER OF THE CORRECT ANSWER IN THE SPACE AT THE RIGHT.*

1. The one of the following situations in which you as a supervisor of a group of clerks would probably be able to function MOST effectively from the viewpoint of departmental efficiency is where you are responsible DIRECTLY to
   A. a single supervisor having sole jurisdiction over you
   B. two or three supervisors having coordinate jurisdiction over you
   C. four or five supervisors having coordinate jurisdiction over you
   D. all individuals of higher rank than you in the department

   1.____

2. Suppose that it is necessary to order one of the clerks under your supervision to stay overtime a few hours one evening. The work to be done is not especially difficult. It is the custom in your office to make such assignments by rotation. The particular clerk whose turn it is to work overtime requests to be excused that evening, but offers to work the next time that overtime is necessary. Hitherto, this clerk has always been very cooperative.
   Of the following, the BEST action for you to take is to
   A. grant the clerk's request, but require her to work overtime two additional nights to compensate for this concession
   B. inform the clerk that you are compelled to refuse any request for special consideration
   C. grant the clerk's request if another clerk is willing to substitute for her
   D. refuse the clerk's request outright because granting her request may encourage her to evade other responsibilities

   2.____

3. When asked to comment upon the efficiency of Miss Jones, a clerk, her supervisor said, "Since she rarely makes an error, I consider her very efficient."
   Of the following, the MOST valid assumption underlying this supervisor's comment is that
   A. speed and accuracy should be considered separately in evaluating a clerk's efficiency
   B. the most accurate clerks are not necessarily the most efficient
   C. accuracy and competency are directly related
   D. accuracy is largely dependent upon the intelligence of a clerk

   3.____

4. The one of the following which is the MOST accurate statement of one of the functions of a supervisor is to
   A. select scientifically the person best fitted for the specific job to be done
   B. train the clerks assigned to you in the best methods of doing the work of your office
   C. fit the job to be done to the clerks who are available
   D. assign a clerk only to those tasks for which she has the necessary experience

5. Assume that you, an experienced supervisor, are given a newly appointed clerk to assist you in performing a certain task. The new clerk presents a method of doing the task which is different from your method but which is obviously better and easy to adopt.
   Of the following you, the supervisor, should
   A. take the suggestion and try it out, even though it was offered by someone less experienced
   B. reject the idea, even though it appears an improvement, as it very likely would not work out
   C. send the new clerk away and get someone else to assist who will be more in accord with your ideas
   D. report him to the head of the office and ask that the new clerk be instructed to do things your way

6. As a supervisor, you should realize that the one of the following general abilities of a junior clerk which is probably LEAST susceptible to improvement by practice and training is
   A. intelligence
   B. speed of typing
   C. knowledge of office procedures
   D. accuracy of filing

7. As a supervisor, when training an employee, you should NOT
   A. correct errors as he makes them
   B. give him too much material to absorb at one time
   C. have him try the operation until he can do it perfectly
   D. treat any foolish question seriously

8. If a supervisor cannot check readily all the work in her unit, she should
   A. hold up the work until she can personally check it
   B. refuse to take additional work
   C. work overtime until she can personally finish it
   D. delegate part of the work to a qualified subordinate

9. The one of the following over which a unit supervisor has the LEAST control is
   A. the quality of the work done in his unit
   B. the nature of the work handled in his unit
   C. the morale of workers in his unit
   D. increasing efficiency of his unit

10. Suppose that you have received a note from an important official in your department commending the work of a unit of clerks under your supervision. Of the following, the BEST action for you to take is to
    A. withhold the note for possible use at a time when the morale of the unit appears to be declining
    B. show the note only to the better members of your staff as a reward for their good work
    C. show the note only to the poorer members of your staff as a stimulus for better work
    D. post the note conspicuously so that it can be seen by all members of your staff

10._____

11. If you find that one of your subordinates is becoming apathetic towards his work, you should
    A. prefer charges against him
    B. change the type of work
    C. request his transfer
    D. advise him to take a medical examination to check his health

11._____

12. Suppose that a new clerk has been assigned to the unit which you supervise. To give this clerk a brief picture of the functioning of your unit in the entire department would be
    A. *commendable*, because she will probably be able to perform her work with more understanding
    B. *undesirable*, because such action will probably serve only to confuse her
    C. *commendable*, because, if transferred, she would probably be able to work efficiently without additional training
    D. *undesirable*, because in-service training has been demonstrated to be less efficient than on-the-job training

12._____

13. Written instructions to a subordinate are of value because they
    A. can be kept up-to-date   B. encourage initiative
    C. make a job seem easier   D. are an aid in training

13._____

14. Suppose that you have assigned a task to a clerk under your supervision and have given appropriate instructions. After a reasonable period, you check her work and find that one specific aspect of her work is consistently incorrect. Of the following, the BEST action for you to take is to
    A. determine whether the clerk has correctly understood instructions concerning the aspect of the work not being done correctly
    B. assign the task to a more competent clerk
    C. wait for the clerk to commit a more flagrant error before taking up the matter with her
    D. indicate to the clerk that you are dissatisfied with her work and wait to see whether she is sufficiently intelligent to correct her own mistakes

14._____

15. If you wanted to check on the accuracy of the filing in your unit, you would
    A. check all the files thoroughly at regular intervals
    B. watch the clerks while they are filing
    C. glance through filed papers at random
    D. inspect thoroughly a small section of the files selected at random

16. In making job assignments to his subordinates, a supervisor should follow the principle that each individual generally is capable of
    A. performing one type of work well and less capable of performing other types well
    B. learning to perform a wide variety of different types of work
    C. performing best the type of work in which he has had least experience
    D. learning to perform any type of work in which he is given training

17. Of the following, the information that is generally considered MOST essential in a departmental organization survey chart is the
    A. detailed operations of the department
    B. lines of authority
    C. relations of the department to other departments
    D. names of the employees of the department

18. Suppose you are the supervisor in charge of a large unit in which all of the clerical staff perform similar tasks.
    In evaluating the relative accuracy of the clerks, the clerk who should be considered to be the LEAST accurate is the one
    A. whose errors result in the greatest financial loss
    B. whose errors cost the most to locate
    C. who makes the greatest percentage of errors in his work
    D. who makes the greatest number of errors in the unit

19. Aside from requirements imposed by authority, the frequency with which reports are submitted or the length of the interval which they cover should depend PRINCIPALLY on the
    A. availability of the data to be included in the reports
    B. amount of time required to prepare the reports
    C. extent of the variations in the data with the passage of time
    D. degree of comprehensiveness required in the reports

20. A serious error has been discovered by a critical superior in work carried on under your supervision.
    It is BEST to explain the situation and prevent its recurrence by
    A. claiming that you are not responsible because you do not check the work personally
    B. accepting the complaint and reporting the name of the employee responsible for the error
    C. assuring him that you hope it will not occur again
    D. assuring him that you will find out how it occurred, so that you can have the work checked with greater care in the future

21. A serious procedural problem develops in your office.
In your solution of this problem, the very FIRST step to take is to
    A. select the personnel to help you
    B. analyze your problem
    C. devise the one best method of research
    D. develop an outline of your report

22. Your office staff consists of eight clerks, stenographers, and typists, cramped in a long narrow room. The room is very difficult to ventilate properly, and, as in so many other offices, the disagreement over the method of ventilation is marked. Two cliques are developing and the friction is carrying over into the work of the office.
Of the following, the BEST way to proceed is to
    A. call your staff together, have the matter fully discussed giving each person an opportunity to be heard, and put the matter to a vote; then enforce the method of ventilation which has the most votes
    B. call your staff together and have the matter fully discussed. If a compromise arrangement is agreed upon, put it into effect. Otherwise, on the basis of all the facts at your disposal, make a decision as to how best to ventilate the room and enforce your decision
    C. speak to the employees individually, make a decision as to how to ventilate the room, and then enforce your decision
    D. study the layout of the office, make a decision as to how best to ventilate the room, and then enforce your decision

23. An organization consisting of six levels of authority, where eight persons are assigned to each supervisor on each level, would consist of APPROXIMATELY _____ persons.
    A. 50   B. 500   C. 5,000   D. 50,000

24. The one of the following which is considered by political scientists to be a GOOD principle of municipal government is
    A. concentration of authority and responsibility
    B. the long ballot
    C. low salaries and a narrow range in salaries
    D. short terms for elected city officials

25. Of the following, the statement concerning the organization of a department which is TRUE is:
    A. In general, no one employee should have active and constant supervision over more than ten persons.
    B. It is basically unwise to have a supervisor with only three subordinates.
    C. It is desirable that there be no personal contact between the rank and file employee and the supervisor once removed from him.
    D. There should be no more than four levels of authority between the top administrative office in a department and the rank and file employees.

26. Assuming that Dictaphones are not available, of the following, the situation in which it would be MOST desirable to establish a central stenographic unit is one in which the unit would serve
    A. ten correspondence clerks assigned to full-time positions answering correspondence of a large government department
    B. seven members of a government commission heading a large department
    C. seven heads of bureaus in a government department consisting of 250 employees
    D. fifty investigators in a large department

27. You are assigned to review the procedures in an office in order to recommend improvements to the commissioner directly. You go into an office performing seen routine operations in the processing of one type of office form.
    The question you should FIRST ask yourself in your study of any one of these operations is:
    A. Can it be simplified?
    B. Is it necessary?
    C. Is it performed in proper order or should its position in the procedure be changed?
    D. Is the equipment for doing it satisfactory?

28. You are assigned in charge of a clerical bureau performing a single operation. All five of your subordinates do exactly the same work. A fine spirit of cooperation has developed and the employees help each other and pool their completed work so that the work of any one employee is indistinguishable. Your office is very busy and all five clerks are doing a full day's work. However, reports come back to you from other offices that they are finding as much as 1% error in the work of your bureau. This is too high a percentage of error.
    Of the following, the BEST procedure for you to follow is to
    A. check all the work yourself
    B. have a sample of the work of each clerk checked by another clerk
    C. have all work done in your office checked by one of your clerks
    D. identify the work of each clerk in some way

29. You are put in charge of a small office. In order to cover the office during the lunch hour, you assign Employee A to remain in the office between the hours of 12 and 1 P.M. On your return to the office at 12:25 P.M., you note that no one is in the office and that the phone is ringing. You are forced to postpone your 12:30 P.M. luncheon appointment, and to remain in the office until 12:50 P.M. when Employee A returns to the office.
    The BEST of the following actions is:
    A. Ask Employee why he left the office
    B. Bring charges against Employee A for insubordination and neglect of duty
    C. Ignore the matter in your conversation with Employee A so as not to embarrass him
    D. Make a note to rate Employee A low on his service rating

30. You are assigned in charge of a large division. It had been the practice in that division for the employees to slip out for breakfast about 10:00 A.M. You had been successful in stopping this practice and for one week no one had gone out for breakfast. One day a stenographer comes over to you at 10:30 A.M. appearing to be ill. She states that she doesn't feel well and that she would like to go out for a cup of tea. She asks your permission to leave the office for a few minutes.
You should
    A. telephone and have a cup of tea delivered to her
    B. permit her to go out
    C. refuse her permission to go out inasmuch as this would be setting a bad example
    D. tell her she can leave for an early lunch hour

31. The following four remarks from a supervisor to a subordinate deal with different situations. One remark, however, implies a basically POOR supervisory practice.
Select this remark as your answer.
    A. "I've called the staff together primarily because I am displeased with the work which one of you is doing. John, don't you think you should be ashamed that you are spoiling the good work of the office?"
    B. "James, you have been with us for six months now. In general, I'm satisfied with your work. However, don't you think you could be more neat in your appearance? I also want you to try to be more accurate in your work."
    C. "Joe, when I assigned this job to you, I did it because it requires special care and I think you're one of our best men in this type of work, but here is a slip-up you've made that we should be especially careful to watch out for in the future."
    D. "Tim, first I'd like to tell you that, effective tomorrow, you are to be my assistant and will receive an increase in salary. Although I recommended you for this position because I felt that you are the best man for the job, there are some things about your work which could stand a bit of improvement. For instance, your manner with regard to visitors is not so polite as it could be."

32. Of the following, the BEST type of floor surface for an office is
    A. concrete   B. hardwood   C. linoleum   D. parquet

33. The GENERALLY accepted unit for the measurement of illumination at a desk or work bench is the
    A. ampere   B. foot-candle   C. volt   D. watt

34. The one of the following who is MOST closely allied with "scientific management" is
    A. Mosher   B. Probst   C. Taylor   D. White

35. Eliminating slack in work assignments is
    A. speed-up
    B. time study
    C. motion study
    D. efficient management

36. "Time studies" examine and measure
    A. past performance
    B. present performance
    C. long-run effect
    D. influence of change

37. The maximum number of subordinates who can be effectively supervised by one supervisor is BEST considered as
    A. determined by the law of "span of control"
    B. determined by the law of "span of attention"
    C. determined by the type of work supervised
    D. fixed at not more than six

38. In the theory and practice of public administration, the one of the following which is LEAST generally regarded as a staff function is
    A. budgeting
    B. firefighting
    C. purchasing
    D. research and information

39. Suppose you are part of an administrative structure in which the executive head has regularly reporting directly to him seventeen subordinates. To some of the subordinates there regularly report directly three employees, to others four employees, and to the remaining subordinates five employees.
    Called upon to make a suggestion concerning this organization, you would question FIRST the desirability of
    A. so large a variation among the number of employees regularly reporting directly to subordinates
    B. having so large a number of subordinates regularly reporting directly to the administrative head
    C. so small a variation among the number of employees regularly reporting directly to subordinates
    D. the hierarchical arrangement

40. Administration is the center but not necessarily the source of all ideas for procedural improvement.
    The MOST significant implication that this principle bears for the administrative officer is that
    A. before procedural improvements are introduced, they should be approved by a majority of the staff
    B. it is the unique function of the administrative officer to derive and introduce procedural improvements
    C. the administrative office should derive ideas and suggestions for procedural improvement from all possible sources, introducing any that promise to be effective
    D. the administrative officer should view employee grievances as the chief source of procedural improvements

41. The merit system should not end with the appointment of a candidate. In any worthy public service system there should be no dead-end jobs. If the best citizen is to be attracted to public service, there must be provided encouragement and incentive to enable such a career employee to progress in the service.
The one of the following which is the MOST accurate statement on the basis of the above statement is that
    A. merit system selection has replaced political appointment in many governmental units
    B. lack of opportunities for advancement in government employment will discourage the better qualified from applying
    C. employees who want to progress in the public service should avoid simple assignments
    D. most dead-end jobs have been eliminated from the public service

41._____

42. Frequently the importance of keeping office records is not appreciated until information which is badly needed cannot be found. Office records must be kept in convenient and legible form, and must be filed where they may be found quickly. Many clerks are required for this work in large offices and fixed standards of accomplishment often can and must be utilized to get the desired results without loss of time.
The one of the following which is the MOST accurate statement on the basis of the above statement is:
    A. In setting up a filing system, the system to be used is secondary to the purpose it is to serve.
    B. Office records to be valuable must be kept in duplicate.
    C. The application of work standards to certain clerical functions frequently leads to greater efficiency.
    D. The keeping of office records becomes increasingly important as the business transacted by an office grows.

42._____

43. The difference between the average worker and the expert in any occupation is to a large degree a matter of training, yet the difference in their output is enormous. Despite this fact, there are many offices which do not have any organized system of training.
The MOST accurate of the following statements on the basis of the above statement is that
    A. job training, to be valuable, should be a continuous process
    B. most clerks have the same general intelligence but differ only in the amount of training they have received
    C. skill in an occupation can be acquired as a result of instruction by others
    D. employees with similar training will produce similar quality and quantity of work

43._____

44. Sometimes the term "clerical work" is used synonymously with the term "office work" to indicate that the work is clerical work, whether done by a clerk in a place called "the office," by the foreman in the shop, or by an investigator in the field. The essential feature is the work itself, not who does it or where it is done. If it is clerical work in one place, it is clerical work everywhere.

44._____

Of the following, the LEAST DIRECT implication of the above statement is that
- A. many jobs have clerical aspects
- B. some clerical work is done in offices
- C. the term "clerical work" is used in place of the term "office work" to emphasize the nature of the work done rather than by whom it is done
- D. clerks are not called upon to perform other than clerical work

45. Scheduling work within a unit involves the knowledge of how long the component parts of the routine take, and the precedence which certain routines should take over others. Usually, the important functions should be attended to on a schedule, and less important work can be handled as fill-in.
The one of the following which is the VALID statement on the basis of the above statement is that
- A. only employees engaged in routine assignments should have their work scheduled
- B. the work of an employee should be so scheduled that occasional absences will not upset his routine
- C. a proper scheduling of work takes the importance of the various functions of a unit into consideration
- D. if office work is not properly scheduled, important functions will be neglected

45.____

46. A filing system is unquestionably an effective tool for the systematic executive, and it use in office practice is indispensable, but a casual examination of almost any filing drawer in any office will show that hundreds of letters and papers which have no value whatever are being preserved.
The LEAST accurate of the following statements on the basis of the above statement is that
- A. it is generally considered to be good office practice to destroy letters or papers which are of no value
- B. many files are cluttered with useless paper
- C. a filing system is a valuable aid in effective office management
- D. every office executive should personally make a thorough examination of the files at regular intervals

46.____

47. As a supervisor, you may receive requests for information which you know should not be divulged.
Of the following replies you may give to such a request received over the telephone, the BEST one is:
- A. "I regret to advise you that it is the policy of the department not to give out this information over the telephone."
- B. "If you hold on a moment, I'll have you connected with the chief of the division."
- C. "I am sorry that I cannot help you, but we are not permitted to give out any information regarding such matters."
- D. "I am sorry but I know nothing regarding this matter."

47.____

48. Training promotes cooperation and teamwork, and results in lowered unit costs of operation.
The one of the following which is the MOST valid implication of the above statement is that
   A. training is of most value to new employees
   B. training is a factor in increasing efficiency and morale
   C. the actual cost of training employees may be small
   D. training is unnecessary in offices where personnel costs cannot be reduced

49. A government employee should understand how his particular duties contribute to the achievement of the objectives of his department.
This statement means MOST NEARLY that
   A. an employee who understands the functions of his department will perform his work efficiently
   B. all employees contribute equally in carrying out the objectives of their department
   C. an employee should realize the significance of his work in relation to the aims of his department
   D. all employees should be able to assist in setting up the objectives of a department

50. Many office managers have a tendency to overuse form letters and are prone to print form letters for every occasion, regardless of the number of copies of these letters which is needed.
On the basis of this statement, it is MOST logical to state that the determination of the need for a form letter should depend upon the
   A. length of the period during which the form letter may be used
   B. number of form letters presently being used in the office
   C. frequency with which the form letter may be used
   D. number of typists who may use the form letter

KEY (CORRECT ANSWERS)

1. A	11. B	21. B	31. A	41. B
2. C	12. A	22. B	32. C	42. C
3. C	13. D	23. A	33. B	43. C
4. B	14. A	24. A	34. C	44. D
5. A	15. D	25. D	35. D	45. C
6. A	16. B	26. D	36. B	46. D
7. B	17. B	27. B	37. C	47. C
8. D	18. C	28. D	38. B	48. B
9. B	19. C	29. A	39. B	49. C
10. D	20. D	30. B	40. C	50. C

TEST 2

DIRECTIONS: Each question or incomplete statement is followed by several suggested answers or completions. Select the one that BEST answers the question or completes the statement. *PRINT THE LETTER OF THE CORRECT ANSWER IN THE SPACE AT THE RIGHT.*

1. Your bureau is assigned an important task.
   Of the following, the function that you, as an administrative officer, can LEAST reasonably be expected to perform under these circumstances is the
   A. division of the large job into individual tasks
   B. establishment of "production lines" within the bureau
   C. performance personally of a substantial share of all the work
   D. checkup to see that the work has been well done

2. Suppose that you have broken a complex job into its smaller components before making assignments to the employees under your jurisdiction.
   Of the following, the LEAST advisable procedure to follow from that point is to
   A. give each employee a picture of the importance of his work for the success of the total job
   B. establish a definite line of work flow and responsibility
   C. post a written memorandum of the best method for performing each job
   D. teach a number of alternative methods for doing each job

3. As an administrative officer, you are requested to draw up an organization chart of the whole department.
   Of the following, the MOST important characteristic of such a chart is that it will
   A. include all details of the organization which distinguish it from any other
   B. be a schematic representation of purely administrative functions within the department
   C. present a modification of the actual departmental organization in light of principles of scientific management
   D. present an accurate picture of the lines of authority and responsibility

4. Of the following, the MOST important principle in respect to delegation of authority that should guide you in your work as supervisor in charge of a bureau is that you should
   A. delegate as much authority as you effectively can
   B. make certain that all administrative details clear through your desk
   C. have all decisions confirmed by you
   D. discourage the practice of consulting you on matters of basic policy

5. Of the following, the LEAST valid criterion to be applied in evaluating the organization of the department in which you are employed as a supervisor is:
   A. Is authority for making decisions centralized?
   B. Is authority for formulating policy centralized?
   C. Is authority granted commensurate with the responsibility involved?
   D. Is each position and its relation to other positions from the standpoint of responsibility clearly defined?

2 (#2)

6. Functional centralization is the bringing together of employees doing the same kind of work and performing similar tasks.
Of the following, the one which is NOT an important advantage flowing from the introduction of functional centralization in a large city department is that
   A. inter-bureau communication and traffic are reduced
   B. standardized work procedures are introduced more easily
   C. evaluation of employee performances is facilitated
   D. inequalities in working conditions are reduced

7. As a supervisor, you find that a probationary employee under your supervision is consistently below a reasonable standard of performance for the job he is assigned to do.
Of the following, the MOST appropriate action for you to take FIRST is to
   A. give him an easier job to do
   B. advise him to transfer to another department
   C. recommend to your superior that he be discouraged at the end of his probationary period
   D. determine whether the cause for his below-standard performance can be readily remedied

8. Certain administrative functions, such as those concerned with budgetary and personnel selection activities, have been delegated to central agencies separated from the operating departments.
Of the following, the PRINCIPAL reason for such separation is that
   A. a central agency is generally better able to secure funds for performing these functions
   B. decentralization increases executive control
   C. greater economy, efficiency, and uniformity can be obtained by establishing central staff of experts to perform these functions
   D. the problems involved in performing these functions vary significantly from one operating department to another

9. The one of the following which is LEAST valid as a guiding principle for you, in your work as supervisor, in building team spirit and teamwork in your bureau is that you should attempt to
   A. convince the personnel of the bureau that public administration is a worthwhile endeavor
   B. lead every employee to visualize the integration of his own individual function with the program of the whole bureau
   C. develop a favorable public attitude toward the work of the bureau
   D. maintain impartiality by convenient delegation of authority in controversial matters

10. Of the following, the LEAST desirable procedure for the competent supervisor to follow is to
    A. organize his work before taking responsibility for helping others with theirs
    B. avoid schedules and routines when he is busy
    C. be flexible in planning and carrying out his responsibilities
    D. secure the support of his staff in organizing the total job of the unit

11. The responsibility for making judgment about staff members which is inherent in the supervisor's position may arouse hostilities toward the supervisor.
    Of the following, the BEST suggestion to the supervisor for handling this responsibility is for the supervisor to avoid
    A. individual criticism by taking up problems directly through group meetings
    B. any personal feeling or action that would imply that the supervisor has any power over the staff
    C. making critical judgments without accompanying them with reassurance to the staff member concerned

12. To carry out MOST effectively his responsibility for holding to a standard of quantity and quality, the supervisor should
    A. demand much more from himself than he does from his staff
    B. provide a clearly defined statement of what is expected of the staff
    C. teach the staff to assume responsible attitudes
    D. help the staff out when they get into unavoidable difficulties

13. The supervisor should inspire confidence and respect.
    This objective is MOST likely to be attained by the supervisor if he endeavors always to
    A. know the answers to the workers' questions
    B. be fair and just
    C. know what is going on in the office
    D. behave like a supervisor

14. Two chief reasons for the centralization of office functions are to eliminate costly duplication and to bring about greater coordination.
    The MOST direct implication of this statement is that
    A. greater coordination of office work will result in centralization of office functions
    B. where there is no centralization of office functions, there can be no coordination of work
    C. centralization of office functions may reduce duplication of work
    D. decentralization of office functions may be a result of costly duplication

15. The efficient administrative assistant arranges a definite schedule of the regular work of his division, but assigns the occasional and emergency tasks when they arise to the employees available at the time to handle these tasks.
    The management procedure described in this statement is desirable MAINLY because it
    A. relieves the administrative assistant of the responsibility of supervising the work of his staff
    B. enables more of the staff to become experienced in handling different types of problems
    C. enables the administrative assistant to anticipate problems which may arise
    D. provides for consideration of current work load when making special assignments

4 (#2)

16. Well-organized training courses for office employees are regarded by most administrators as a fundamental and essential part of a well-balanced personnel program.
Such training of clerical employees results LEAST directly in
    A. providing a reservoir of trained employees who can carry on the duties of other clerks during the absence of these clerks
    B. reducing the individual differences in the innate ability of clerical employees to perform complex duties
    C. bringing about a standardization throughout the department of operational methods found to be highly effective in one of its units
    D. preparing clerical employees for promotion to more responsible positions

17. The average typing speed of a typist is not necessarily a true indication of her efficiency.
Of the following, the BEST justification for this statement is that
    A. the typist may not maintain her maximum typing speed at all times
    B. a rapid typist will ordinarily type more letters than a slow one
    C. a typist's assignments usually include other operations in addition to actual typing
    D. typing speed has no significant relationship to the difficulty of material being typed

18. Although the use of labor-saving machinery and the simplification of procedures tend to decrease unit clerical labor costs, there is, nevertheless, a contrary tendency in the overall cost of office work. This contrary tendency, evidenced by the increase in size of the office staffs, has developed from the increasingly extensive use of systems of analysis and methods of research.
Of the following, the MOST accurate statement on the basis of the above statement is that
    A. the tendency for the overall costs of office work to increase is bringing about a counter-tendency to decrease unit costs of office work
    B. office machines are of little value in reducing the unit costs of the work of offices in which the overall costs are increasing
    C. The increasing use of systems of analysis and methods of research is bringing about a condition which will necessitate a curtailment of the use of these techniques in the office
    D. expanded office functions tend to offset savings resulting from increased efficiency in office management

19. The most successful supervisor wins his victories through preventive rather than through curative action.
The one of the following which is the MOST accurate statement on the basis of this statement is that
    A. success in supervision may be measured more accurately in terms of errors corrected than in terms of errors prevented
    B. anticipating problems makes for better supervision than waiting until these problems arise

C. difficulties that cannot be prevented by the supervisor cannot be overcome
D. the solution of problems in supervision is best achieved by scientific methods

20. Assume that you have been requested to design an office form which is to be duplicated by the mimeograph process.
In planning the layout of the various items appearing on the form, it is LEAST important for you to know the
    A. amount of information which the form is to contain
    B. purpose for which the form will be used
    C. size of the form
    D. number of copies of the form which are required

20._____

21. The supervisor is responsible for the accuracy of the work performed by her subordinates.
Of the following procedures which she might adopt to insure the accurate copying of long reports from rough draft originals, the MOST effective one is to
    A. examine the rough draft for errors in grammar, punctuation, and spelling before assigning it to a typist to copy
    B. glance through each typed report before it leaves her bureau to detect any obvious errors made by the typist
    C. have another employee read the rough draft original to the typist who typed the report, and have the typist make whatever corrections are necessary
    D. rotate assignments involving the typing of long reports equally among all the typists in the unit

21._____

22. The total number of errors made during the month, or other period studied, indicates, in a general way, whether the work has been performed with reasonable accuracy. However, this is not in itself a true measure, but must be considered in relation to the total volume of work produced.
On the basis of this statement, the accuracy of work performed is MOST truly measured by the
    A. total number of errors made during a specified period
    B. comparison of the number of errors made and the quantity of work produced during a specified period
    C. average amount of work produced by the unit during each month or other designated period of time
    D. none of the above answers

22._____

23. In the course of your duties, you receive a letter which, you believe, should be called to the attention of your supervisor.
Of the following, the BEST reason for attaching previous correspondence to this letter before giving it to your supervisor is that
    A. there is less danger, if such a procedure is followed, of misplacing important letters
    B. this letter can probably be better understood in the light of previous correspondence

23._____

C. your supervisor is probably in a better position to understand the letter than you
D. this letter will have to be filed eventually so there is no additional work involved

24. Suppose that you are requested to transmit to the stenographers in your bureau an order curtailing certain privileges that they have been enjoying. You anticipate that your staff may resent curtailment of such privileges.
Of the following, the BEST action for you to take is to
   A. impress upon your staff that an order is an order and must be obeyed
   B. attempt to explain to your staff the probable reasons for curtailing their privileges
   C. excuse the curtailment of privileges by saying that the welfare of the staff was evidently not considered
   D. warn your staff that violation of an order may be considered sufficient cause for immediate dismissal

24.____

25. Suppose that a stenographer recently appointed to your bureau submits a memorandum suggesting a change in office procedure that has been tried before and has been found unsuccessful.
Of the following, the BEST action for you to take is to
   A. send the stenographer a note acknowledging receipt of the suggestion, but do not attempt to carry out the suggestion
   B. point out that suggestions should come from her supervisor, who has a better knowledge of the problems of the office
   C. try out the suggested change a second time, lest the stenographer lose interest in her work
   D. call the stenographer in, explain that the change if not practicable, and compliment her for her interest and alertness

25.____

26. Suppose that you are assistant to one of the important administrators in your department. You receive a note from the head of department asking your supervisor to assist with a pressing problem that has arisen by making an immediate recommendation. Your supervisor is out of town on official business for a few days and cannot be reached. The head of department, evidently, is not aware of his absence.
Of the following, the BEST action for you to take is to
   A. send the note back to the head of department without comment so as not to incriminate your supervisor
   B. forward the note to one of the administrators in another division of the department
   C. wait until your supervisor returns and bring the note to his attention immediately
   D. get in touch with the head of department immediately and inform him that your supervisor is out of town

26.____

27. One of your duties may be to estimate the budget of your unit for the next fiscal year. Suppose that you expect no important changes in the work of your unit during the next year.

27.____

Of the following, the MOST appropriate basis for estimating next year's budget is the
- A. average budget of your unit for the last five years
- B. budget of your unit for the current year plus fifty percent to allow for possible expansion
- C. average current budget of units in your department
- D. budget of your unit for the current fiscal year

28. As a supervisor, you should realize that the work of a stenographer ordinarily requires a higher level of intelligence than the work of a typist CHIEFLY because
    - A. the salary range of stenographers is, in most government and business offices, lower than the salary range of typists
    - B. greater accuracy and skill is ordinarily required of a typist
    - C. the stenographer must understand what is being dictated to enable her to write it out in shorthand
    - D. typists are required to do more technical and specialized work

29. Suppose that you are acting as assistant to an important administrator in your department.
    Of the following, the BEST reason for keeping a separate "pending" file of letters to which answers are expected very soon is that
    - A. important correspondence should be placed in a separate, readily accessible file
    - B. a periodic check of the "pending" file will indicate the possible need for follow-up letters
    - C. correspondence is never final, so provision should be made for keeping files open
    - D. there is seldom sufficient room in the permanent files to permit filing all letters

30. For a busy executive in a government department, the services of an assistant are valuable and almost indispensable.
    Of the following, the CHIEF value of an assistant PROBABLY lies in her
    - A. ability to assume responsibility for making major decisions
    - B. familiarity with the general purpose and functions of civil service
    - C. special education
    - D. familiarity with the work and detail involved in the duties of the executive whom she assists

31. The supervisor should set a good example.
    Of the following, the CHIEF implication of the above statement is that the supervisor should
    - A. behave as he expects his workers to behave
    - B. know as much about the worker as his workers do
    - C. keep his workers informed of what he is doing
    - D. keep ahead of his workers

32. Of the following, the LEAST desirable procedure for the competent supervisor to follow is to
    A. organize his work before taking responsibility for helping others with theirs
    B. avoid schedules and routines when he is busy
    C. be flexible in planning and carrying out his responsibilities
    D. secure the support of his staff in organizing the total job of the unit

33. Evaluation helps the worker by increasing his security.
    Of the following, the BEST justification for this statement is that
    A. security and growth depend upon knowledge by the worker of the agency's evaluation
    B. knowledge of his evaluation by agency and supervisor will stimulate the worker to better performance
    C. evaluation enables the supervisor and worker to determine the reasons for the worker's strengths and weaknesses
    D. the supervisor and worker together can usually recognize and deal with any worker's insecurity

34. Systematizing for efficiency means MOST NEARLY
    A. performing an assignment despite all interruptions
    B. leaving difficult assignments until the next day
    C. having a definite time schedule for certain daily duties
    D. trying to do as little work as possible

35. The CHIEF reason for an employee training program is to
    A. increase the efficiency of the employee's work
    B. train the employee for promotion examinations
    C. to meet and talk with each new employee
    D. to give the supervisor an opportunity to reprimand the employee for his lack of knowledge

36. A supervisor may encourage his subordinates to make suggestions by
    A. keeping a record of the number of suggestions an employee makes
    B. providing a suggestion box
    C. outlining a list of possible suggestions
    D. giving credit to a subordinate whose suggestion has been accepted and used

37. The statement that accuracy is of greater importation than speed means MOST NEARLY that
    A. slower work increases employment
    B. fast workers may be inferior workers
    C. there are many varieties of work to do in an office
    D. the slow worker is the most efficient person

38. To print tabular material is always much more expensive than to print straight text.
It follows MOST NEARLY that
   A. the more columns and subdivisions there are in a table, the more expensive is the printing
   B. the omission of the number and title from a table reduces printing costs
   C. it is always desirable to only print straight text
   D. do not print tabular material as it is too expensive

39. If you were required to give service ratings to employees under your supervision, you should consider as MOST important, during the current period, the
   A. personal characteristics and salary and grade of an employee
   B. length of service and the volume of work performed
   C. previous service rating given him
   D. personal characteristics and the quality of work of an employee

40. If a representative committee of employees in a large department is to meet with an administrative officer for the purpose of improving staff relations and of handling grievances, it is BEST that these meetings be held
   A. at regular intervals
   B. whenever requested b an aggrieved employee
   C. whenever the need arises
   D. at the discretion of the administrative officer

41. In order to be best able to teach a newly appointed employee who must learn to do a type of work which is unfamiliar to him, his supervisor should realize that during this first stage in the learning process the subordinate is GENERALLY characterized by
   A. acute consciousness of self
   B. acute consciousness of subject matter, with little interest in persons or personalities
   C. inertness or passive acceptance of assigned role
   D. understanding of problems without understanding of the means of solving them

42. The MOST accurate of the following principles of education and learning for a supervisor to keep in mind when planning a training program for the assistant supervisors under her supervision is that
   A. assistant supervisors, like all other individuals, vary in the rate at which they learn new material and in the degree to which they can retain what they do learn
   B. experienced assistant supervisors who have the same basic college education and agency experience will be able to learn new material at approximately the same rate of speed
   C. the speed with which assistant supervisors can learn new material after the age of forty is half as rapid as at ages twenty to thirty
   D. with regard to any specific task, it is easier and takes less time to break an experienced assistant supervisor of old, unsatisfactory work habits than it is to teach him new, acceptable ones

43. A supervisor has been transferred from supervision of one group of units to another group of units in the same center. She spends the first three weeks in her new assignment in getting acquainted with her new subordinates, their caseload problems and their work. In this process, she notices that some of the cash records and forms which are submitted to her by two of the assistant supervisors are carelessly or improperly prepared.
The BEST of the following actions for the supervisor to take in this situation is to
   A. carefully check the work submitted by these assistant supervisors during an additional three weeks before taking any more positive action
   B. confer with these offending workers and show each one where her work needs improvement and how to go about achieving it
   C. institute an in-service training program specifically designed to solve such a problem and instruct the entire subordinate staff in proper work methods
   D. make a note of these errors for documentary use in preparing the annual service rating reports and advise the workers involved to prepare their work more carefully

43.____

44. A supervisor, who was promoted to this position a year ago, has supervised a certain assistant supervisor for this one year. The work of the assistant supervisor has been very poor because he has done a minimum of work, refused to take sufficient responsibility, been difficult to handle, and required very close supervision. Apparently due to the increasing insistence by his supervisor that he improve the caliber of his work, the assistant supervisor tenders his resignation, stating that the demands of the job are too much for him. The opinion of the previous supervisor, who had supervised this assistant supervisor for two years, agrees substantially with that of the new supervisor. Under such circumstances, the BEST of the following actions the supervisor can take, in general, is to
   A. recommend that the resignation be accepted and that he be rehired should he later apply when he feels able to do the job
   B. recommend that the resignation be accepted and that he not be rehired should he later so apply
   C. refuse to accept the resignation but try to persuade the assistant supervisor to accept psychiatric help
   D. refuse to accept the resignation, promising the assistant supervisor that he will be less closely supervised in the future since he is now so experienced

44.____

45. Rumors have arisen to the effect that one of the staff investigators under your supervision has been attending classes at a local university during afternoon hours when he is supposed to be making field visits.
The BEST of the following ways for you to approach this problem is to
   A. disregard the rumors since, like most rumors, they probably have no actual foundation in fact
   B. have a discreet investigation made in order to determine the actual facts prior to taking any other action

45.____

C. inform the investigator that you know what he has been doing and that such behavior is overt dereliction of duty and is punishable by dismissal
D. review the investigator's work record, spot check his cases, and take no further action unless the quality of his work is below average for the unit

46. A supervisor must consider many factors in evaluating a worker whom he has supervised for a considerable time.
In evaluating the capacity of such a worker to use independent judgment, the one of the following to which the supervisor should generally give MOST consideration is the worker's
   A. capacity to establish good relationships with people (clients, colleagues)
   B. educational background
   C. emotional stability
   D. the quality and judgment shown by the worker in previous work situations known to the supervisor

46._____

47. A supervisor is conducting a special meeting with the assistant supervisors under her supervision to read and discuss some major complex changes in the rules and procedures. She notices that one of the assistant supervisors who is normally attentive at meetings seems to be paying no attention to what is being said. The supervisor stops reading the rules and asks the assistant supervisor a couple of questions about the changed procedure, to which she gets satisfactory answers.
The BEST action of the following for the supervisor to take at the meeting is to
   A. advise the assistant supervisor gently but firmly that these changes are complex and that her undivided attention is required in order to fully comprehend them
   B. avoid further embarrassment to the assistant supervisor by asking the group as a whole to pay more attention to what is being read
   C. discontinue the questioning and resume reading the procedure
   D. politely request the assistant supervisor to stop giving those present the impression that she is uninterested in what goes on about her

47._____

48. A supervisor becomes aware that one of her very competent experienced workers never takes notes during an interview with a client except to note an occasional name, address, or date. When asked about this practice by the supervisor, the worker states that she has a good memory for important details and has always been able to satisfactorily record an interview after the client has left.
It would generally be BEST for the supervisor to handle this situation by
   A. discussing with her that more extensive note-taking may sometimes be desirable with a client who believes note-taking to be evidence that his problem will receive serious consideration
   B. agreeing with this practice since note-taking interferes with the establishment of a proper worker-client relationship
   C. explaining that, since interviewing is an art form rather than an exact science, a good worker must devise her own personal rules for interviewing and not be bound by general principles

48._____

D. warning the worker that memory is too uncertain a thing to be relied upon and, therefore, notes should be taken during an interview of all matters

49. When an experienced subordinate who has the authority and information necessary to make a decision on a certain difficult matter brings the matter to his supervisor without having made the decision, it would generally be BEST for the supervisor to
    A. agree to make the decision for the subordinate after the subordinate has explained why he finds it difficult to make the decision and after he has made a recommendation
    B. make the decision for the subordinate, explaining to him the reasons for arriving at the decision
    C. refuse to make the decision, but discuss the various alternatives with the subordinate in order to clarify the issues involved
    D. refuse to make the decision, explaining to the subordinate that he is deemed to be fully qualified and competent to make the decision

49.____

50. The one of the following instances when it is MOST important for an upper level supervisor to follow the chain of command is when he is
    A. communicating decisions   B. communicating information
    C. receiving suggestions   D. seeking information

50.____

KEY (CORRECT ANSWERS)

1.	C	11.	D	21.	C	31.	A	41.	A
2.	D	12.	B	22.	B	32.	B	42.	A
3.	D	13.	B	23.	B	33.	C	43.	B
4.	A	14.	C	24.	B	34.	C	44.	B
5.	D	15.	D	25.	D	35.	A	45.	B
6.	A	16.	B	26.	D	36.	D	46.	D
7.	D	17.	C	27.	D	37.	B	47.	C
8.	C	18.	D	28.	C	38.	A	48.	A
9.	D	19.	B	29.	B	39.	D	49.	C
10.	B	20.	D	30.	D	40.	A	50.	A

TEST 3

DIRECTIONS: Each question or incomplete statement is followed by several suggested answers or completions. Select the one that BEST answers the question or completes the statement. *PRINT THE LETTER OF THE CORRECT ANSWER IN THE SPACE AT THE RIGHT.*

1. Experts in the field of personnel relations feel that it is generally bad practice for subordinate employees to become aware of pending or contemplated changes in policy or organizational set-up via the "grapevine" CHIEFLY because
    A. evidence that one or more responsible officials have proved untrustworthy will undermine confidence in the agency
    B. the information disseminated by this method is seldom entirely accurate and generally spreads needless unrest among the subordinate staff
    C. the subordinate staff may conclude that the administration feels the staff cannot be trusted with the true information
    D. the subordinate staff may conclude that the administration lacks the courage to make an unpopular announcement through officials channels

1.____

2. In order to maintain a proper relationship with a worker who is assigned to staff rather than line functions, a line supervisor should
    A. accept all recommendations of the staff worker
    B. include the staff worker in the conferences called by the supervisor for his subordinates
    C. keep the staff worker informed of developments in the area of his staff assignment
    D. require that the staff worker's recommendations be communicated to the supervisor through the supervisor's own superior

2.____

3. Of the following, the GREATEST disadvantage of placing a worker in a staff position under the direct supervision of the supervisor whom he advises is the possibility that the
    A. staff worker will tend to be insubordinate because of a feeling of superiority over the supervisor
    B. staff worker will tend to give advice of the type which the supervisor wants to hear or finds acceptable
    C. supervisor will tend to be mistrustful of the advice of a worker of subordinate rank
    D. supervisor will tend to derive little benefit from the advice because to supervise properly he should know at least as much as his subordinate

3.____

4. One factor which might be given consideration in deciding upon the optimum span of control of a supervisor over his immediate subordinates is the position of the supervisor in the hierarchy of the organization. It is generally considered proper that the number of subordinates immediately supervised by a higher, upper echelon, supervisor
    A. is unrelated to and tends to form no pattern with the number supervised by lower level supervisors
    B. should be about the same as the number supervised by a lower level supervisor

4.____

C. should be larger than the number supervised by a lower level supervisor
D. should be smaller than the number supervised by a lower level supervisor

5. An important administrative problem is how precisely to define the limits on authority that is delegated to subordinate supervisors.
Such definition of limits of authority should be
   A. as precise as possible and practicable in all areas
   B. as precise as possible and practicable in areas of function, but should allow considerable flexibility in the area of personnel management
   C. as precise as possible and practicable in the area of personnel management, but should allow considerable flexibility in the areas of function
   D. in general terms so as to allow considerable flexibility both in the areas of function and in the areas of personnel management

6. The LEAST important of the following reasons why a particular activity should be assigned to a unit which performs activities dissimilar to it is that
   A. close coordination is needed between the particular activity and other activities performed by the unit
   B. it will enhance the reputation and prestige of the unit supervisor
   C. the unit makes frequent use of the results of this particular activity
   D. the unit supervisor has a sound knowledge and understanding of the particular activity

7. A supervisor is put in charge of a special unit. She is exceptionally well-qualified for this assignment by her training and experience. One of her very close personal friends has been working for some time as a field investigator in this unit. Both the supervisor and investigator are certain that the rest of the investigators in the unit, many of whom have been in the bureau for a long time, know of this close relationship.
Under these circumstances, the MOST advisable action for the supervisor to take is to
   A. ask that either she be allowed to return to her old assignment, or, if that cannot be arranged, that her friend be transferred to another unit in the center
   B. avoid any overt sign of favoritism by acting impartially and with greater reserve when dealing with this investigator than the rest of the staff
   C. discontinue any socializing with this investigator either inside or outside the office so as to eliminate any gossip or dissatisfaction
   D. talk the situation over with the other investigators and arrive at a mutually acceptable plan of proper office decorum

8. The one of the following causes of clerical error which is usually considered to be LEAST attributable to faulty supervision or inefficient management is
   A. inability to carry out instructions
   B. too much work to do
   C. an inappropriate record-keeping system
   D. continual interruptions

9. Assume that you are the supervisor of a clerical unit in a government agency. One of your subordinates violates a rule of the agency, a violation which requires that the employee be suspended from his work for one day. The violated rule is one that you have found to be unduly strict and you have recommended to the management of the agency that the rule be changed or abolished. The management has been considering your recommendation but has not yet reached a decision on the matter.
In these circumstances, you should
   A. not initiate disciplinary action, but, instead explain to the employee that the rule may be changed shortly
   B. delay disciplinary action on the violation until the management has reached a decision on changing the rule
   C. modify the disciplinary action by reprimanding the employee and informing him that further action may be taken when the management has reached a decision on changing the rule
   D. initiate the prescribed disciplinary action without commenting on the strictness of the rule or on your recommendation

10. Assume that a supervisor praises his subordinates for satisfactory aspects of their work only when he is about to criticize them for unsatisfactory aspects of their work.
Such a practice is undesirable PRIMARILY because
   A. his subordinates may expect to be praised for their work even if it is unsatisfactory
   B. praising his subordinates for some aspects of their work while criticizing other aspects will weaken the effects of the criticisms
   C. his subordinates would be more receptive to criticism if it were followed by praise
   D. his subordinates may come to disregard praise and wait for criticism to be given

11. The one of the following which would be the BEST reason for an agency to eliminate a procedure for obtaining and recording certain information is that
   A. it is no longer legally required to obtain the information
   B. there is an advantage in obtaining the information
   C. the information could be compiled on the basis of other information available
   D. the information obtained is sometimes incorrect

12. In determining the type and number of records to be kept in an agency, it is important to recognize that records are of value PRIMARILY as
   A. raw material to be used in statistical analysis
   B. sources of information about the agency's activities
   C. by-products of the activities carried on by the agency
   D. data for evaluating the effectiveness of the agency

Questions 13-17.

DIRECTIONS: Each of Questions 13 through 17 consists of a statement which contains one word that is incorrectly used because it is not in keeping with the meaning that the statement is evidently intended to convey. For each of these questions, you are to select the incorrectly used word and substitute for it one of the words lettered A, B, C, or D, which helps BEST to convey the meaning of the statement.

13. There has developed in recent years an increasing awareness of the need to measure the quality of management in all enterprises and to seek the principles that can serve as a basis for this improvement.
     A. growth   B. raise   C. efficiency   D. define

14. It is hardly an exaggeration to deny that the permanence, productivity, and humanity of any industrial system depend upon its ability to utilize the positive and constructive impulses of all who work and upon its ability to arouse and continue interest in the necessary activities.
     A. develop   B. efficiency   C. state   D. inspiration

15. The selection of managers on the basis of technical knowledge alone seems to recognize that the essential characteristic of management is getting things done through others, thereby demanding skills that are essential in coordinating the activities of subordinates.
     A. training
     B. fails
     C. organization
     D. improving

16. Only when it is deliberate and when it is clearly understood what impressions the ease of communication will probably create in the minds of employees and subordinate management, should top management refrain from commenting on a subject that is of general concern.
     A. obvious   B. benefit   C. doubt   D. absence

17. Scientific planning of work requires careful analysis of facts and a precise plan of action for the whims and fancies of executives that often provide only a vague indication of work to be done.
     A. substitutes
     B. development
     C. preliminary
     D. comprehensive

18. Assume that you are a supervisor. One of the workers under your supervision is careless about the routine aspects of his work.
    Of the following, the action MOST likely to develop in this worker a better attitude toward job routines is to demonstrate that
     A. it is just as easy to do his job the right way
     B. organization of his job will leave more time for field work
     C. the routine part of the job is essential to performing a good piece of work
     D. job routines are a responsibility of the worker

19. A supervisor can MOST effectively secure necessary improvement in a worker's office work by
    A. encouraging the worker to keep abreast of his work
    B. relating the routine part of his job to the total job to be done
    C. helping the worker to establish a good system for covering his office work and holding him to it
    D. informing the worker that he will be required to organize his work more efficiently

20. A supervisor should offer criticism in such a manner that the criticisms is helpful and not overwhelming.
    Of the following, the LEAST valid inference that can be drawn on the basis of the above statement is that a supervisor should
    A. demonstrate that the criticism is partial and not total
    B. give criticism in such a way that it does not undermine the worker's self-confidence
    C. keep his relationships with the worker objective
    D. keep criticism directed towards general work performance

21. The one of the following areas in which a worker may LEAST reasonably expect direct assistance from the supervisor is in
    A. building up rapport with all clients
    B. gaining insight into the unmet needs of clients
    C. developing an understanding of community resources
    D. interpreting agency policies and procedures

22. You are informed that a worker under your supervision has submitted a letter complaining of unfair service rating.
    Of the following, the MOST valid assumption for you to make concerning this worker is that he should be
    A. more adequately supervised in the future
    B. called in for a supervisory conference
    C. given a transfer to some other unit where he may be more happy
    D. given no more consideration than any other inefficient worker

23. Assume that you are a supervisor. You find that a somewhat bewildered worker, newly appointed to the department, hesitates to ask questions for fear of showing his ignorance and jeopardizing his position.
    Of the following, the BEST procedure for you to follow is to
    A. try to discover the reason for his evident fear of authority
    B. tell him that when he is in doubt about a procedure or a policy he should consult his fellow workers
    C. develop with the worker a plan for more frequent supervisory conferences
    D. explain why each staff member is eager to give him available information that will help him do a good job

24. Of the following, the MOST effective method of helping a newly-appointed employee adjust to his new job is to
    A. assure him that with experience his uncertain attitudes will be replaced by a professional approach
    B. help him, by accepting him as he is, to have confidence in his ability to handle the job
    C. help him to be on guard against the development of punitive attitudes
    D. help him to recognize the mutability of the agency's policies and procedures

25. Suppose that, as a supervisor, you have scheduled an individual conference with an experienced employee under your supervision.
    Of the following, the BEST plan of action for this conference is to
    A. discuss the work that the employee is most interested in
    B. plan with the employee to cover any problems that are difficult for him
    C. advise the employee that the conference is his to do with as he sees fit
    D. spot check the employee's work in advance and select those areas for discussion in which the employee has done poor work

26. Of the following, the CHIEF function of a supervisor should be to
    A. assist in the planning of new policies and the evaluation of existing ones
    B. promote congenial relationships among members of the staff
    C. achieve optimum functioning of each unit and each worker
    D. promote the smooth functioning of job routines

27. The competent supervisor must realize the importance of planning.
    Of the following, the aspect of planning which is LEAST appropriately considered a responsibility of the supervisor is
    A. long-range planning for the proper functioning of his unit
    B. planning to take care of peak and slack periods
    C. planning to cover agency policies in group conferences
    D. long-range planning to develop community resources

28. The one of the following objectives which should be of LEAST concern to the supervisor in the performance of his duties is to
    A. help the worker to make friends with all of his fellow employees
    B. be impartial and fair to all members of the staff
    C. stimulate the worker's growth on the job
    D. meet the needs of the individual employee

29. The one of the following which is LEAST properly considered a direct responsibility of the supervisor is
    A. liaison between the staff and the administrator
    B. interpreting administrative orders and procedures to the employees
    C. training new employees
    D. maintaining staff morale at a high level

30. In order to teach the employee to develop an objective approach, the BEST action for the supervisor to take is to help the worker to
    A. develop a sincere interest in his job
    B. understand the varied responsibilities that are an integral part of his job
    C. differentiate clearly between himself as a friend and as an employee
    D. find satisfaction in his work

31. If the employee shows excessive submission which indicates a need for dependence on the supervisor in handling an assignment, it would be MOST advisable for the supervisor to
    A. indicate firmly that the employee-supervisor relationship does not call for submission
    B. define areas of responsibility of employee and supervisor
    C. recognize the employee's need and of supervisor
    D. recognize the employee's need to be sustained and supported and help him by making decisions for him

32. Assume that, as a supervisor, you are conducting a group conference.
    Of the following, the BEST procedure for you to follow in order to stimulate group discussion is to
    A. permit the active participation of all members
    B. direct the discussion to an acceptable conclusion
    C. resolve conflicts of opinion among members of the group
    D. present a question for discussion on which the group members have some knowledge or experience

33. Suppose that, as a new supervisor, you wish to inform the staff under your supervision of your methods of operation.
    Of the following, the BEST procedure for you to follow is to
    A. advise the staff that they will learn gradually from experience
    B. inform each employee in an individual conference
    C. call a group conference for this purpose
    D. distribute a written memorandum among all members of the staff

34. The MOST constructive and effective method of correcting an employee who has made a mistake is, in general, to
    A. explain that his evaluation is related to his errors
    B. point out immediately where he erred and tell him how it should have been done
    C. show him how to readjust his methods so as to avoid similar errors in the future
    D. try to discover by an indirect method why the error was made

35. The MOST effective method for the supervisor to follow in order to obtain the cooperation of an employee under his supervision is, wherever possible, to
    A. maintain a careful record of performance in order to keep the employee on his toes
    B. give the employee recognition in order to promote greater effort and give him more satisfaction in his work

C. try to gain the employee's cooperation for the good of the service
D. advise the employee that his advancement on the job depends on his cooperation

36. Of the following, the MOST appropriate initial course for an employee to take when he is unable to clarify a policy with his supervisor is to
    A. bring up the problem at the next group conference
    B. discuss the policy immediately with his fellow employees
    C. accept the supervisor's interpretation as final
    D. determine what responsibility he has for putting the policy into effect

37. Good administration allows for different treatment of different workers. Of the following, the CHIEF implication of this statement is that
    A. it would be unfair for the supervisor not to treat all staff members alike
    B. fear of favoritism tends to undermine staff morale
    C. best results are obtained by individualization within the limits of fair treatment
    D. difficult problems call for a different kind of approach

38. The MOST effective and appropriate method of building efficiency and morale in a group of employees is, in general,
    A. by stressing the economic motive
    B. through use of the authority inherent in the position
    C. by a friendly approach to all
    D. by a discipline that is fair but strict

39. Of the following, the LEAST valid basis for the assignment of work to an employee is the
    A. kind of service to be rendered
    B. experience and training of the employee
    C. health and capacity of the employee
    D. racial composition of the community where the office is located

40. The CHIEF justification for staff education, consisting of in-service training, lies in its contribution to
    A. improvement in the quality of work performed
    B. recruitment of a better type of employee
    C. employee morale, accruing from a feeling of growth on the job
    D. the satisfaction that the employee gets on his job

41. Suppose that you are a supervisor. An employee no longer with your department requests you, as his former supervisor, to write a letter recommending him for a position with a private organization.
Of the following the BEST procedure for you to follow is to include in the letter only information that
    A. will help the applicant get the job
    B. is clear, factual, and substantiated
    C. is known to you personally
    D. can readily be corroborated by personal interview

42. Of the following, the MOST important item on which to base the efficiency evaluation of an employee under your supervision is
    A. the nature of the relationship that he has built up with his fellow employees
    B. how he gets along with his supervisors
    C. his personal habits and skills
    D. the effectiveness of his control over his work

43. According to generally accepted personnel practice, the MOST effective method of building morale in a new employee is to
    A. exercise caution in praising the employee, lest he become overconfident
    B. give sincere and frank recommendation whenever possible in order to stimulate interest and effort
    C. praise the employee highly even for mediocre performance so that he will be stimulated to do better
    D. warn the employee frequently that he cannot hope to succeed unless he puts forth his best efforts

44. Errors made by newly-appointed employees often follow a predictable pattern. The one of the following errors likely to have LEAST serious consequences is the tendency of a new employee to
    A. discuss problems that are outside his province with the client
    B. persuade the client to accept the worker's solution of a problem
    C. be two strict in carrying out departmental policy and procedure
    D. depend upon the use of authority due to his inexperience and lack of skill in working with people

45. The MOST effective way for a supervisor to break down a worker's defensive stand against supervisory guidance is to
    A. come to an understanding with him on the mutual responsibilities involved in the job of the employee and that of the supervisor
    B. tell him he must feel free to express his opinions and to discuss basic problems
    C. show him how to develop toward greater objectivity, sensitivity, and understanding
    D. advise him that it is necessary to carry out agency policy and procedures in order to do a good job

46. Of the following, the LEAST essential function of the supervisor who is conducting a group conference should be to
    A. keep attention focused on the purpose of the conference
    B. encourage discussion of controversial points
    C. make certain that all possible viewpoints are discussed
    D. be thoroughly prepared in advance

47. When conducting a group conference, the supervisor should be LEAST concerned with
    A. providing an opportunity for the free interchange of ideas
    B. imparting knowledge and understanding of the work

C. leading the discussion toward a planned goal
D. pointing out where individual workers have erred in work practice

48. If the participants in a group conference are unable to agree on the proper application of a concept to the work of a department, the MOST suitable temporary procedure for the supervisor to follow is to
    A. suggest that each member think the subject through before the next meeting
    B. tell the group to examine their differences for possible conflicts with present policies
    C. suggest that practices can be changed because of new conditions
    D. state the acceptable practice in the agency and whether deviations from such practice can be permitted

49. If an employee is to participate constructively in any group discussion, it is MOST important that he have
    A. advance notice of the agenda for the meeting
    B. long experience in the department
    C. knowledge and experience in the particular work
    D. the ability to assume a leadership role

50. Of the following, the MOST important principle for the supervisor to follow when conducting a group discussion is that he should
    A. move the discussion toward acceptance by the group of a particular point of view
    B. express his ideas clearly and succinctly
    C. lead the group to accept the authority inherent in his position
    D. contribute to the discussion from his knowledge and experience

KEY (CORRECT ANSWERS)

1.	B	11.	C	21.	A	31.	B	41.	B
2.	C	12.	B	22.	B	32.	D	42.	D
3.	B	13.	B	23.	C	33.	C	43.	B
4.	D	14.	C	24.	B	34.	C	44.	C
5.	A	15.	B	25.	B	35.	B	45.	A
6.	B	16.	D	26.	C	36.	D	46.	B
7.	A	17.	A	27.	D	37.	C	47.	D
8.	A	18.	D	28.	A	38.	D	48.	D
9.	D	19.	B	29.	A	39.	D	49.	A
10.	D	20.	D	30.	C	40.	A	50.	D

NAME AND NUMBER COMPARISONS

COMMENTARY

This test seeks to measure your ability and disposition to do a job carefully and accurately, your attention to exactness and preciseness of detail, your alertness and versatility in discerning similarities and differences between things, and your power in systematically handling written language symbols.

It is actually a test of your ability to do academic and/or clerical work, using the basic elements of verbal (qualitative) and mathematical (quantitative) learning—words and numbers.

EXAMINATION SECTION

TEST 1

DIRECTIONS: In each line across the page there are three names or numbers that are much alike. Compare the three names or numbers and decide which ones are exactly alike. *PRINT IN THE SPACE AT THE RIGHT THE LETTER:*
   A. if all THREE names or numbers are exactly alike
   B. if only the FIRST and SECOND names or numbers are ALIKE
   C. if only the FIRST and THIRD names or numbers are alike
   D. if only the SECOND or THIRD names or numbers are alike
   E. if ALL THREE names or numbers are DIFFERENT

1.	Davis Hazen	David Hozen	David Hazen	1.____
2.	Lois Appel	Lois Appel	Lois Apfel	2.____
3.	June Allan	Jane Allan	Jane Allan	3.____
4.	10235	10235	10235	4.____
5.	32614	32164	32614	5.____

TEST 2

1.	2395890	2395890	2395890	1.____
2.	1926341	1926347	1926314	2.____
3.	E. Owens McVey	E. Owen McVey	E. Owen McVay	3.____
4.	Emily Neal Rouse	Emily Neal Rowse	Emily Neal Rowse	4.____
5.	H. Merritt Audubon	H. Merriott Audubon	H. Merritt Audubon	5.____

2

TEST 3

1. 6219354	6219354	6219354	1.____
2. 231793	2312793	2312793	2.____
3. 1065407	1065407	1065047	3.____
4. Francis Ransdell	Frances Ramsdell	Francis Ramsdell	4.____
5. Cornelius Detwiler	Cornelius Detwiler	Cornelius Detwiler	5.____

TEST 4

1. 6452054	6452564	6542054	1.____
2. 8501268	8501268	8501286	2.____
3. Ella Burk Newham	Ella Burk Newnham	Elena Burk Newnham	3.____
4. Jno. K. Ravencroft	Jno. H. Ravencroft	Jno. H. Ravencoft	4.____
5. Martin Wills Pullen	Martin Wills Pulen	Martin Wills Pullen	5.____

TEST 5

1. 3457988	3457986	3457986	1.____
2. 4695682	4695862	4695682	2.____
3. Stricklund Kaneydy	Sticklund Kanedy	Stricklund Kanedy	3.____
4. Joy Harlor Witner	Joy Harloe Witner	Joy Harloe Witner	4.____
5. R.M.O. Uberroth	R.M.O. Uberroth	R.N.O. Uberroth	5.____

3

TEST 6

1. 1592514	1592574	1592574	1.____
2. 2010202	2010202	2010220	2.____
3. 6177396	6177936	6177396	3.____
4. Drusilla S. Ridgeley	Drusilla S. Ridgeley	Drusilla S. Ridgeley	4.____
5. Andrei I. Tooumantzev	Andrei I. Tourmantzev	Andrei I. Toumantzov	5.____

TEST 7

1. 5261383	5261383	5261338	1.____
2. 8125690	8126690	8125609	2.____
3. W.E. Johnston	W.E. Johnson	W.E. Johnson	3.____
4. Vergil L. Muller	Vergil L. Muller	Vergil L. Muller	4.____
5. Atherton R. Warde	Asheton R. Warde	Atherton P. Warde	5.____

TEST 8

1. 013469.5	023469.5	02346.95	1.____
2. 33376	333766	333766	2.____
3. Ling-Temco-Vought	Ling-Tenco-Vought	Ling-Temco Vought	3.____
4. Lorilard Corp.	Lorillard Corp.	Lorrilard Corp.	4.____
5. American Agronomics Corporation	American Agronomics Corporation	American Agronomic Corporation	5.____

TEST 9

1.	436592864	436592864	436592864	1.____
2.	197765123	197755123	197755123	2.____
3.	Dewaay Cortvriendt International S.A.	Deway Cortvriendt International S.A.	Deway Corturiendt International S.A.	3.____
4.	Crédit Lyonnais	Crèdit Lyonnais	Crèdit Lyonais	4.____
5.	Algemene Bank Nederland N.V.	Algamene Bank Nederland N.V.	Algemene Bank Naderland N.V.	5.____

TEST 10

1.	00032572	0.0032572	00032522	1.____
2.	399745	399745	398745	2.____
3.	Banca Privata Finanziaria S.p.A.	Banca Privata Finanzaria S.P.A.	Banca Privata Finanziaria S.P.A.	3.____
4.	Eastman Dillon, Union Securities & Co.	Eastman Dillon, Union Securities Co.	Eastman Dillon, Union Securities & Co.	4.____
5.	Arnhold and S. Bleichroeder, Inc.	Arnhold & S. Bleichroeder, Inc.	Arnold and S. Bleichroeder, Inc.	5.____

TEST 11

DIRECTIONS: Answer the questions below on the basis of the following instructions: For each such numbered set of names, addresses, and numbers listed in Columns I and II, select your answer from the following options:
A. The names in Columns I and II are different
B. The addresses in Columns I and II are different
C. The numbers in Columns I and II are different
D. The names, addresses and numbers are identical

1. Francis Jones
   62 Stately Avenue
   96-12446

   Francis Jones
   62 Stately Avenue
   96-21446

   1.____

2. Julio Montez
   19 Ponderosa Road
   56-73161

   Julio Montez
   19 Ponderosa Road
   56-71361

   2.____

3. Mary Mitchell
   2314 Melbourne Drive
   68-92172

   Mary Mitchell
   2314 Melbourne Drive
   68-92172

   3.____

4. Harry Patterson
   25 Dunne Street
   14-33430

   Harry Patterson
   25 Dunne Street
   14-34330

   4.____

5. Patrick Murphy
   171 West Hosmer Street
   93-81214

   Patrick Murphy
   171 West Hosmer Street
   93-18214

   5.____

TEST 12

1. August Schultz
816 St. Clair Avenue
53-40149

   August Schultz
816 St. Claire Avenue
53-40149

   1.____

2. George Taft
72 Runnymede Street
47-04033

   George Taft
72 Runnymede Street
47-04023

   2.____

3. Angus Henderson
1418 Madison Street
81-76375

   Angus Henderson
1418 Madison Street
81-76375

   3.____

4. Carolyn Mazur
12 Rivenlew Road
38-99615

   Carolyn Mazur
12 Rivervane Road
38-99615

   4.____

5. Adele Russell
1725 Lansing Lane
72-91962

   Adela Russell
1725 Lansing Lane
72-91962

   5.____

TEST 13

DIRECTIONS: The following questions are based on the instructions given below. In each of the following questions, the 3-line name and address in Column I is the master-list entry, and the 3-line entry in Column II is the information to be checked against the master list.
If there is one line that is NOT exactly alike, mark your answer A.
If there are two lines NOT exactly alike, mark your answer B.
If there are three lines NOT exactly alike, mark your answer C.
If the lines ALL are exactly alike, mark your answer D.

1. Jerome A. Jackson   Jerome A. Johnson   1.____
   1243 14th Avenue   1234 14th Avenue
   New York, N.Y. 10023   New York, N.Y. 10023

2. Sophie Strachtheim   Sophie Strachtheim   2.____
   33-28 Connecticut Ave.   33-28 Connecticut Ave.
   Far Rockaway, N.Y. 11697   Far Rockaway, N.Y. 11697

3. Elisabeth NT. Gorrell   Elizabeth NT. Correll   3.____
   256 Exchange St   256 Exchange St.
   New York, N.Y. 10013   New York, N.Y. 10013

4. Maria J. Gonzalez   Maria J. Gonzalez   4.____
   7516 E. Sheepshead Rd.   7516 N. Shepshead Rd.
   Brooklyn, N.Y. 11240   Brooklyn, N.Y. 11240

5. Leslie B. Brautenweiler   Leslie B. Brautenwieler   5.____
   21-57A Seller Terr.   21-75ASeiler Terr.
   Flushing, N.Y. 11367   Flushing, N.J. 11367

KEY (CORRECT ANSWERS)

TEST 1	TEST 2	TEST 3	TEST 4	TEST 5	TEST 6	TEST 7
1. E	1. A	1. A	1. E	1. D	1. D	1. B
2. B	2. E	2. A	2. B	2. C	2. B	2. E
3. D	3. E	3. B	3. E	3. E	3. C	3. D
4. A	4. D	4. E	4. E	4. D	4. A	4. A
5. C	5. C	5. A	5. C	5. B	5. E	5. E

TEST 8	TEST 9	TEST 10	TEST 11	TEST 12	TEST 13
1. E	1. A	1. E	1. C	1. B	1. B
2. D	2. D	2. B	2. C	2. C	2. D
3. E	3. E	3. E	3. D	3. D	3. A
4. E	4. E	4. C	4. C	4. B	4. A
5. B	5. E	5. E	5. C	5. A	5. C

NAME AND NUMBER CHECKING
EXAMINATION SECTION
TEST 1

DIRECTIONS: Questions 1 through 17 consist of sets of names and addresses. In each question, the name and address in Column II should be an exact copy of the name and address in Column I.
If there is:
a mistake only in the name, mark your answer A;
a mistake only in the address, mark your answer B;
a mistake in both name and address, mark your answer C;
No mistake in either name or address, mark your answer D.

Sample Question

Column I
Christina Magnusson
288 Greene Street
New York, N.Y. 10003

Column II
Christina Magnusson
288 Greene Street
New York, N.Y. 10013

Since there is a mistake only in the address (the zip code should be 10003 instead of 10013), the answer to the sample question is B.

COLUMN I

1. Ms. Joan Kelly
   313 Franklin Avenue
   Brooklyn, N.Y. 11202

2. Mrs. Eileen Engel
   47-24 86 Road
   Queens, N.Y. 11122

3. Marcia Michaels
   213 E. 81 St.
   New York, N.Y. 10012

4. Rev. Edward J. Smyth
   1401 Brandeis Street
   San Francisco, Calif. 96201

5. Alicia Rodriguez
   24-68 82 St.
   Elmhurst, N.Y. 11122

COLUMN II

1. Ms. Joan Kielly
   318 Franklin Ave.
   Brooklyn, N.Y. 11202

2. Mrs. Ellen Engel
   47-24 86 Road
   Queens, New York 11122

3. Marcia Michaels
   213 E. 81 St.
   New York, N.Y. 10012

4. Rev. Edward J. Smyth
   1401 Brandies Street
   San Francisco, Calif. 96201

5. Alicia Rodriguez
   2468 81 St.
   Elmhurst, N.Y. 11122

1.____
2.____
3.____
4.____
5.____

2 (#1)

COLUMN I	COLUMN II	
6. Ernest Eisemann 21 Columbia St. New York, N.Y. 10007	Ernest Eisermann 21 Columbia St. New York, N.Y. 10007	6. ____
7. Mr. & Mrs. George Petersson 87-11 91st Avenue Woodhaven, N.Y. 11421	Mr. & Mrs. George Peterson 87-11 91st Avenue Woodhaven, N.Y. 11421	7. ____
8. Mr. Ivan Klebnikov 1848 Newkirk Avenue Brooklyn, N.Y. 11226	Mr. Ivan Klebikov 1848 Newkirk Avenue Brooklyn, N.Y. 11622	8. ____
9. Mr. Samuel Rothfleisch 71 Pine Street New York, N.Y. 10005	Samuel Rothfleisch 71 Pine Street New York, N.Y. 100005	9. ____
10. Mrs. Isabel Tonnessen 198 East 185th Street Bronx, N.Y. 10458	Mrs. Isabel Tonnessen 189 East 185th Street Bronx, N.Y. 10348	10. ____
11. Esteban Perez 173 Eighth Street Staten Island, N.Y. 10306	Estaban Perez 173 Eighth Street Staten Island, N.Y. 10306	11. ____
12. Esta Wong 141 West 68 St. New York, N.Y. 10023	Esta Wang 141 West 68 St. New York, N.Y. 10023	12. ____
13. Dr. Alberto Grosso 3475 12th Avenue Brooklyn, N.Y. 11218	Dr. Alberto Grosso 3475 12th Avenue Brooklyn, N.Y. 11218	13. ____
14. Mrs. Ruth Bortias 482 Theresa Ct. Far Rockaway, N.Y. 11691	Ms. Ruth Bortlas 482 Theresa Ct. Far Rockaway, N.Y. 11169	14. ____
15. Mr. & Mrs. Howard Fox 2301 Sedgwick Ave. Bronx, N.Y. 10468	Mr. & Mrs. Howard Fox 231 Sedgwick Ave. Bronx, N.Y. 10468	15. ____
16. Miss Marjorie Black 223 East 23 Street New York, N.Y. 10010	Miss Margorie Black 223 East 23 Street New York, N.Y. 10010	16. ____

3 (#1)

COLUMN I	COLUMN II	
17. Michelle Herman 806 Valley Rd. Old Tappan, N.J. 07675	Michelle Hermann 806 Valley Dr. Old Tappan, N.J. 07675	17.____

KEY (CORRECT ANSWERS)

1.	C	7.	A	13.	D
2.	A	8.	C	14.	C
3.	D	9.	D	15.	B
4.	B	10.	B	16.	A
5.	B	11.	A	17.	C
6.	A	12.	D		

TEST 2

DIRECTIONS: Questions 1 through 15 are to be answered SOLELY on the instructions given below. *PRINT THE LETTER OF THE CORRECT ANSWER IN THE SPACE AT THE RIGHT.*

INSTRUCTIONS

In each of the following questions, the 3-line name and address in Column I is the master-list entry, and the 3-line entry in Column II is the information to be checked against the master list. If there is one line that does not match, mark your answer A; if there are two lines that do not match, mark your answer B; if all three lines do not match, mark your answer C; if the lines all match exactly, mark your answer D.

Sample Question

Column I
Mark L. Field
11-09 Price Park Blvd.
Bronx, N.Y. 11402

Column II
Mark L. Field
11-99 Prince Park Way
Bronx, N.Y. 11401

The first lines in each column match exactly. The second lines do not match since 11-09 does not match 11-99; and Blvd. does not match Way. The third lines do not match either since 11402 does not match 11401. Therefore, there are two lines that do not match, and the CORRECT answer is B.

COLUMN I

1. Jerome A. Jackson
   1243 14th Avenue
   New York, N.Y. 10023

2. Sophie Strachtheim
   33-28 Connecticut Ave.
   Far Rockaway, N.Y. 11697

3. Elisabeth N.T. Gorrell
   256 Exchange St.
   New York, N.Y. 10013

4. Maria J. Gonzalez
   7516 E. Sheepshead Rd.
   Brooklyn, N.Y. 11240

5. Leslie B. Brautenweiler
   21 57A Seiler Terr.
   Flushing, N.Y. 11367

COLUMN II

Jerome A. Johnson
1234 14th Avenuc
New York, N.Y. 10023

Sophie Strachtheim
33-28 Connecticut Ave.
Far Rockaway, N.Y. 11697

Elizabeth N.T. Gorrell
256 Exchange St.
New York, N.Y. 10013

Maria J. Gonzalez
7516 N. Shepshead Rd.
Brooklyn, N.Y. 11240

Leslie B. Brautenwieler
21-75A Seiler Terr.
Flushing, N.J. 11367

1.____
2.____
3.____
4.____
5.____

2 (#2)

COLUMN I	COLUMN II	
6. Rigoberto J. Peredes 157 Twin Towers, #18F Tottenville, S. I., N.Y,	Rigoberto J. Peredes 157 Twin Towers, #18F Tottenville, S.I., N.Y.	6.____
7. Pietro F. Albino P.O. Box 7548 Floral Park, N.Y. 11005	Pietro F. Albina P.O. Box 7458 Floral Park, N.Y. 11005	7.____
8. Joanne Zimmerman Bldg. SW, Room 314 532-4601	Joanne Zimmermann Bldg. SW, Room 314 532-4601	8.____
9. Carlyle Whetstone Payroll Div. –A, Room 212A 262-5000, ext. 471	Carlyle Whetstone Payroll Div. –A, Room 212A 262-5000, ext. 417	9.____
10. Kenneth Chiang Legal Council, Room 9745 (201) 416-9100, ext. 17	Kenneth Chiang Legal Counsel, Room 9745 (201) 416-9100, Ext. 17	10.____
11. Ethel Koenig Personnel Services Division, Room 433; 635-7572	Ethel Hoenig Personal Services Division, Room 433; 635-7527	11.____
12. Joyce Ehrhardt Office of the Administrator, Room W56; 387-8706	Joyce Ehrhart Office of the Administrator, Room W56; 387-7806	12.____
13. Ruth Lang EAM Bldg., Room C101 625-2000, ext. 765	Ruth Lang EAM Bldg., Room C110 625-2000, ext. 765	13.____
14. Anne Marie Ionozzi Investigations, Room 827 576-4000, ext. 832	Anna Marie Ionozzi Investigation, Room 827 566-4000, ext. 832	14.____
15. Willard Jameson Fm C Bldg., Room 687 454-3010	Willard Jamieson Fm C Bldg., Room 687 454-3010	15.____

KEY (CORRECT ANSWERS)

1.	B	6.	D		C
2.	D	7.	B	12.	B
3.	A	8.	D	13.	A
4.	A	9.	B	14.	C
5.	C	10.	A	15.	A

TEST 3

DIRECTIONS: Questions 1 through 10 are to be answered on the basis of the following instructions. *PRINT THE LETTER OF THE CORRECT ANSWER IN THE SPACE AT THE RIGHT.*

<u>INSTRUCTIONS</u>

For each such set of names, addresses, and numbers listed in Columns I and II, select your answer from the following options:
The names in Columns I and II are different,
The addresses in Columns I and II are different,
The numbers in Columns I and II are different,
The names, addresses, and numbers in Columns I and II are identical.

	<u>COLUMN I</u>	<u>COLUMN II</u>	
1.	Francis Jones 62 Stately Avenue 96-12446	Francis Jones 62 Stately Avenue 96-21446	1.____
2.	Julio Montez 19 Ponderosa Road 56-73161	Julio Montez 19 Ponderosa Road 56-71361	2.____
3.	Mary Mitchell 2314 Melbourne Drive 68-92172	Mary Mitchell 2314 Melbourne Drive 68-92172	3.____
4.	Harry Patterson 25 Dunne Street 14-33430	Harry Patterson 25 Dunne Street 14-34330	4.____
5.	Patrick Murphy 171 West Hosmer Street 93-81214	Patrick Murphy 171 West Hosmer Street 93-18214	5.____
6.	August Schultz 816 St. Clair Avenue 53-40149	August Schultz 816 St. Claire Avenue 53-40149	6.____
7.	George Taft 72 Runnymede Street 47-04033	George Taft 72 Runnymede Street 47-04023	7.____
8.	Angus Henderson 1418 Madison Street 81-76375	Angus Henderson 1318 Madison Street 81-76375	8.____

2 (#3)

COLUMN I	COLUMN II	
9. Carolyn Mazur 12 Riverview Road 38-99615	Carolyn Mazur 12 Rivervane Road 38-99615	9.____
10. Adele Russell 1725 Lansing Lane 72-91962	Adela Russell 1725 Lansing Lane 72-91962	10.____

KEY (CORRECT ANSWERS)

1. C   6. B
2. C   7. C
3. D   8. D
4. C   9. B
5. C   10. A

TEST 4

DIRECTIONS: Questions 1 through 20 test how good you are at catching mistakes in typing or printing. In each question, the name and address in Column II should be an exact copy of the name and address in Column I. Mark your answer
  A. If there is no mistake in either name or address;
  B. If there is a mistake in both name and address;
  C. If there is a mistake only in the name;
  D. If there is a mistake only in the address.
PRINT THE LETTER OF THE CORRECT ANSWER IN THE SPACE AT THE RIGHT.

COLUMN I   COLUMN II

1. Milos Yanocek   Milos Yanocek   1.____
    33-60 14 Street   33-60 14 Street
    Long Island City, N.Y. 11011   Long Island City, N.Y. 11001

2. Alphonse Sabattelo   Alphonse Sabbattelo   2.____
    24 Minnetta Lane   24 Minetta Lane
    New York, N.Y. 10006   New York, N.Y. 10006

3. Helen Steam   Helene Stearn   3.____
    5 Metropolitan Oval   5 Metropolitan Oval
    Bronx, N.Y. 10462   Bronx, N.Y. 10462

4. Jacob Weisman   Jacob Weisman   4.____
    231 Francis Lewis Boulevard   231 Francis Lewis Boulevard
    Forest Hills, N.Y. 11325   Forest Hills, N.Y. 11325

5. Riccardo Fuente   Riccardo Fuentes   5.____
    134 West 83 Street   134 West 88 Street
    New York, N.Y. 10024   New York, N.Y. 10024

6. Dennis Lauber   Dennis Lauder   6.____
    52 Avenue D   52 Avenue D
    Brooklyn, N.Y. 11216   Brooklyn, N.Y. 11216

7. Paul Cutter   Paul Cutter   7.____
    195 Galloway Avenue   175 Galloway Avenue
    Staten Island, N.Y. 10356   Staten Island, N.Y. 10365

8. Sean Donnelly   Sean Donnelly   8.____
    45-58 41 Avenue   45-58 41 Avenue
    Woodside, N.Y. 11168   Woodside, N.Y. 11168

9. Clyde Willot   Clyde Willat   9.____
    1483 Rockaway Avenue   1483 Rockaway Avenue
    Brooklyn, N.Y. 11238   Brooklyn, N.Y. 11238

2 (#4)

COLUMN I	COLUMN II	
10. Michael Stanakis 419 Sheriden Avenue Staten Island, N.Y. 10363	Michael Stanakis 419 Sheraden Avenue Staten Island, N.Y. 10363	10.____
11. Joseph DiSilva 63-84 Saunders Road Rego Park, N.Y. 11431	Joseph Disilva 64-83 Saunders Road Rego Park, N.Y. 11431	11.____
12. Linda Polansky 2224 Fendon Avenue Bronx, N.Y. 20464	Linda Polansky 2255 Fenton Avenue Bronx, N.Y. 10464	12.____
13. Alfred Klein 260 Hillside Terrace Staten Island, N.Y. 15545	Alfred Klein 260 Hillside Terrace Staten Island, N.Y. 15545	13.____
14. William McDonnell 504 E. 55 Street New York, N.Y. 10103	William McConnell 504 E. 55 Street New York, N.Y. 10108	14.____
15. Angela Cipolla 41-11 Parson Avenue Flushing, N.Y. 11446	Angela Cipola 41-11 Parsons Avenue Flushing, N.Y. 11446	15.____
16. Julie Sheridan 1212 Ocean Avenue Brooklyn, N.Y. 11237	Julia Sheridan 1212 Ocean Avenue Brooklyn, N.Y. 11237	16.____
17. Arturo Rodriguez 2156 Cruger Avenue Bronx, N.Y. 10446	Arturo Rodrigues 2156 Cruger Avenue Bronx, N.Y. 10446	17.____
18. Helen McCabe 2044 East 19 Street Brooklyn, N.Y. 11204	Helen McCabe 2040 East 19 Street Brooklyn, N.Y. 11204	18.____
19. Charles Martin 526 West 160 Street New York, N.Y. 10022	Charles Martin 526 West 160 Street New York, N.Y. 10022	19.____
20. Morris Rabinowitz 31 Avenue M Brooklyn, N.Y. 11216	Morris Rabinowitz 31 Avenue N Brooklyn, N.Y. 11216	20.____

KEY (CORRECT ANSWERS)

1.	D	11.	B
2.	B	12.	D
3.	C	13.	A
4.	A	14.	B
5.	B	15.	B
6.	C	16.	C
7.	D	17.	C
8.	A	18.	D
9.	B	19.	A
10.	D	20.	D

TEST 5

DIRECTIONS: In copying the addresses below from Column A to the same line in Column B, an Agent-in-Training made some errors. For Questions 1 through 5, if you find that the agent made an error in
only one line, mark your answer A;
only two lines, mark your answer B;
only three lines, mark your answer C;
all four lines, mark your answer D.

EXAMPLE

COLUMN A	COLUMN B
24 Third Avenue	24 Third Avenue
5 Lincoln Road	5 Lincoln Street
50 Central Park West	6 Central Park West
37-21 Queens Boulevard	21-37 Queens Boulevard

Since errors were made on only three lines, namely the second, third, and fourth, the CORRECT answer is C.
PRINT THE LETTER OF THE CORRECT ANSWER IN THE SPACE AT THE RIGHT.

	COLUMN A	COLUMN B	
1.	57-22 Springfield Boulevard 94 Gun Hill Road 8 New Dorp Lane 36 Bedford Avenue	75-22 Springfield Boulevard 94 Gun Hill Avenue 8 New Drop Lane 36 Bedford Avenue	1.____
2.	538 Castle Hill Avenue 54-15 Beach Channel Drive 21 Ralph Avenue 162 Madison Avenue	538 Castle Hill Avenue 54-15 Beach Channel Drive 21 Ralph Avenue 162 Morrison Avenue	2.____
3.	49 Thomas Street 27-21 Northern Blvd. 86 125th Street 872 Atlantic Ave.	49 Thomas Street 21-27 Northern Blvd. 86 125th Street 872 Baltic Ave,	3.____
4.	261-17 Horace Harding Expwy. 191 Fordham Road 6 Victory Blvd. 552 Oceanic Ave.	261-17 Horace Harding Pkwy. 191 Fordham Road 6 Victoria Blvd. 552 Ocean Ave.	4.____
5.	90-05 38th Avenue 19 Central Park West 9281 Avenue X 22 West Farms Square	90-05 36th Avenue 19 Central Park East 9281 Avenue X 22 West Farms Square	5.____

KEY (CORRECT ANSWERS)

1. C
2. A
3. B
4. C
5. B

TEST 6

DIRECTIONS: For Questions 1 through 10, choose the letter in Column II next to the number which EXACTLY matches the number in Column I. *PRINT THE LETTER OF THE CORRECT ANSWER IN THE SPACE AT THE RIGHT.*

COLUMN I COLUMN II

1. 14235
   A. 13254
   B. 12435
   C. 13245
   D. 14235

   1.____

2. 70698
   A. 90768
   B. 60978
   C. 70698]
   D. 70968

   2.____

3. 11698
   A. 11689
   B. 11986
   C. 11968
   D. 11698

   3.____

4. 50497
   A. 50947
   B. 50497
   C. 50749
   D. 54097

   4.____

5. 69635
   A. 60653
   B. 69630
   C. 69365
   D. 69635

   5.____

6. 1201022011
   A. 1201022011
   B. 1201020211
   C. 1202012011
   D. 1021202011

   6.____

7. 3893981389
   A. 3893891389
   B. 3983981389
   C. 3983891389
   D. 3893981389

   7.____

8. 4765476589
   A. 4765476598
   B. 4765476588
   C. 4765476589
   D. 4765746589

   8.____

9. 8679678938
   A. 8679687938
   B. 8679678938
   C. 8697678938
   D. 8678678938
9.____

10. 6834836932
    A. 6834386932
    B. 6834836923
    C. 6843836932
    D. 6834836932
10.____

Questions 11-15.

DIRECTIONS: For Questions 11 through 15, determine how many of the symbols in Column Z are exactly the same as the symbol in Column Y.
If none is exactly the same, answer A;
If only one symbol is exactly the same, answer B;
If two symbols are exactly the same, answer C;
If three symbols are exactly the same, answer D.

COLUMN Y	COLUMN Z	
11. A123B1266	A123B1366 A123B1266 A133B1366 A123B1266	11.____
12. CC28D3377	CD22D3377 CC38D3377 CC28C3377 CC28D2277	12.____
13. M21AB201X	M12AB201X M21AB201X M21AB201Y M21BA201X	13.____
14. PA383Y744	AP383Y744 PA338Y744 PA388Y744 PA383Y774	14.____
15. PB2Y8893	PB2Y8893 PB2Y8893 PB3Y8898 PB2Y8893	15.____

KEY (CORRECT ANSWERS)

1.	D	6.	A	11.	C
2.	C	7.	D	12.	A
3.	D	8.	C	13.	B
4.	B	9.	B	14.	A
5.	D	10.	D	15.	D

CODING

EXAMINATION SECTION

COMMENTARY

An ingenious question-type called coding, involving elements of alphabetizing, filing, name and number comparison, and evaluative judgment and application, has currently won wide acceptance in testing circles for measuring clerical aptitude and general ability, particularly on the senior (middle) grades (levels).

While the directions for this question usually vary in detail, the candidate is generally asked to consider groups of names, codes, and numbers, and then, according to a given plan, to arrange codes in alphabetic order; to arrange these in numerical sequence; to re-arrange columns of names and numbers in correct order; to espy errors in coding; to choose the correct coding arrangement in consonance with the given directions and examples, etc.

This question-type appear to have few parameters in respect to form, substance, or degree of difficulty.

Accordingly, acquaintance with, and practice in, the coding question is recommended for the serious candidate.

TEST 1

DIRECTIONS: Questions 1 through 8 are to be answered on the basis of the code table and the instructions given below.

Code Letter for Traffic Problem	B	H	Q	J	F	L	M	I
Code Number for Action Taken	1	2	3	4	5	6	7	8

Assume that each of the capital letters on the above chart is a radio code for a particular traffic problem and that the number immediately below each capital letter is the radio code for the correct action to be taken to deal with the problem. For instance, "1" is the action to be taken to deal with problem "B", "2" is the action to be taken to deal with problem "H", and so forth.

In each question, a series of code letters is given in Column 1. Column 2 gives four different arrangements of code numbers. You are to pick the answer (A, B, C, or D) in Column 2 that gives the code numbers that match the code letters in the same order.

SAMPLE QUESTION

Column 1
BHLFMQ

Column 2
A. 125678
B. 216573
C. 127653
D. 126573

According to the chart, the code numbers that correspond to these code letters are as follows: B – 1, M – 2, L – 6, F – 5, M – 7, Q – 3. Therefore, the right answer is 126573. This answer is D in Column 2.

2 (#1)

Column 1	Column 2	
1. BHQLMI	A. 123456 B. 123567 C. 123678 D. 125678	1.____
2. HBJQLF	A. 214365 B. 213456 C. 213465 D. 214387	2.____
3. QHMLFJ	A. 321654 B. 345678 C. 327645 D. 327654	3.____
4. FLQJIM	A. 543287 B. 563487 C. 564378 D. 654378	4.____
5. FBIHMJ	A. 518274 B. 152874 C. 528164 D. 517842	5.____
6. MIHFQB	A. 872341 B. 782531 C. 782341 D. 783214	6.____
7. JLFHQIM	A. 465237 B. 456387 C. 4652387 D. 4562387	7.____
8. LBJQIFH	A. 614382 B. 6134852 C. 61437852 D. 61431852	8.____

KEY (CORRECT ANSWERS)

1. C
2. A
3. D
4. B
5. A
6. B
7. C
8. A

TEST 2

DIRECTIONS: Each question or incomplete statement is followed by several suggested answers or completions. Select the one that BEST answers the question or completes the statement. *PRINT THE LETTER OF THE CORRECT ANSWER IN THE SPACE AT THE RIGHT.*

Questions 1-5.

DIRECTIONS: Questions 1 through 5 are based on the following list showing the name and number of each of nine inmates.

1. Johnson   4. Thompson   7. Gordon
2. Smith   5. Frank   8. Porter
3. Edwards   6. Murray   9. Lopez

Each question consists of 3 sets of numbers and letters. Each set should consist of the numbers of three inmates and the first letter of each of their names. The letters should be in the same order as the numbers. In at least two of the three choices, there will be an error. On your answer sheet, mark only that choice in which the letters correspond with the numbers and are in the same order. If all three sets are wrong, mark choice D in your answer space.

SAMPLE QUESTION
A. 386 EPM
B. 542 FST
C. 474 LGT

Since 3 corresponds to E for Edwards, 8 corresponds to P for Porter, and 6 corresponds to M for Murray, choice A is correct and should be entered in your answer space. Choice B is wrong because letters T and S have been reversed. Choice C is wrong because the first number, which is 4, does NOT correspond with the first letter of choice C, which is L. It should have been T. If choice A were also wrong, then D would be the correct answer.

1. A. 382 EGS   B. 461 TMJ   C. 875 PLF   1.____
2. A. 549 FLT   B. 692 MJS   C. 758 GSP   2.____
3. A. 936 LEM   B. 253 FSE   C. 147 JTL   3.____
4. A. 569 PML   B. 716 GJP   C. 842 PTS   4.____
5. A. 356 FEM   B. 198 JPL   C. 637 MEG   5.____

Questions 6-10.

DIRECTIONS: Questions 6 through 10 are to be answered on the basis of the following information:

2 (#3)

In order to make sure stock is properly located, incoming units are stored as follows:

STOCK NUMBERS	BIN NUMBERS
00100 – 39999	D30, L44
40000 – 69999	14L, D38
70000 – 99999	41L, 80D
100000 and over	614, 83D

Using the above table, choose the answer A, B, C, or D, which lists the correct Bin Number for the Stock Number given.

6. 17243
   A. 41L   B. 83D   C. 14L   D. D30   6._____

7. 9219
   A. D38   B. L44   C. 614   D. 41L   7._____

8. 90125
   A. 41L   B. 614   C. D38   D. D30   8._____

9. 10001
   A. L44   B. D38   C. 80D   D. 83D   9._____

10. 200100
    A. 41L   B. 14L   C. 83D   D. D30   10._____

KEY (CORRECT ANSWERS)

1.	B	6.	D
2.	D	7.	B
3.	A	8.	A
4.	C	9.	A
5.	C	10.	C

TEST 3

DIRECTIONS: Each question or incomplete statement is followed by several suggested answers or completions. Select the one that BEST answers the question or completes the statement. *PRINT THE LETTER OF THE CORRECT ANSWER IN THE SPACE AT THE RIGHT.*

Questions 1-9.

DIRECTIONS: Assume that the Police Department is planning to conduct a statistical study of individuals who have been convicted of crimes during a certain year. For the purpose of this study, identification numbers are being assigned to individuals in the following manner:

The first two digits indicate the age of the individual.
The third digit indicates the sex of the individual:
    1. Male
    2. Female
The fourth digit indicates the type of crime involved:
    1. criminal homicide
    2. forcible rape
    3. robbery
    4. aggravated assault
    5. burglary
    6. larceny
    7. auto theft
    8. other
The fifth and sixth digits indicate the month in which the conviction occurred:
    01. January
    02. February, etc.

Questions 1 through 9 are to be answered SOLELY on the basis of the above information and the following list of individuals and identification numbers.

Abbott, Richard	271304	Morris, Chris	212705
Collins, Terry	352111	Owens, William	231412
Elders, Edward	191207	Parker, Leonard	291807
George, Linda	182809	Robinson, Charles	311102
Hill, Leslie	251702	Sands, Jean	202610
Jones, Jackie	301106	Smith, Michael	42108
Lewis, Edith	402406	Turner, Donald	191601
Mack, Helen	332509	White, Barbara	242803

1. The number of women on the above list is
   A. 6   B. 7   C. 8   D. 9

1.____

2. The two convictions which occurred during February were for the crimes of
   A. aggravated assault and auto theft
   B. auto theft and criminal homicide
   C. burglary and larceny
   D. forcible rape and robbery

2._____

3. The ONLY man convicted of auto theft was
   A. Richard Abbott   B. Leslie Hill
   C. Chris Morris   D. Leonard Parker

3._____

4. The number of people on the list who were 25 years old or older is
   A. 6   B. 7   C. 8   D. 9

4._____

5. The OLDEST person on the list is
   A. Terry Collins   B. Edith Lewis
   C. Helen Mack   D. Michael Smith

5._____

6. The two people on the list who are the same age are
   A. Richard Abbott and Michael Smith
   B. Edward Elders and Donald Turner
   C. Linda George and Helen Mack
   D. Leslie Hill and Charles Robinson

6._____

7. A 28-year-old man who was convicted of aggravated assault in October would have identification number
   A. 281410   B. 281509   C. 282311   D. 282409

7._____

8. A 33-year-old woman convicted in April of criminal homicide would have identification number
   A. 331140   B. 331204   C. 332014   D. 332104

8._____

9. The number of people on the above list who were convicted during the first six months of the year is
   A. 6   B. 7   C. 8   D. 9

9._____

Questions 10-19.

DIRECTIONS: The following is a list of patients who were referred by various clinics to the laboratory for tests. After each name is a patient identification number. Questions 10 through 19 are to be answered on the basis of the information contained in this list and the explanation accompanying it.

The first digit refers to the clinic which made the referral:
1. cardiac
2. Renal
3. Pediatrics
4. Ophthalmology
5. Orthopedics
6. Hematology
7. Gynecology
8. Neurology
9. Gastroenterology

The second digit refers to the sex of the patient:
1. male
2. female

The third and fourth digits give the age of the patient

The last two digits give the day of the month the laboratory tests were performed

LABORATORY REFERRALS DURING JANUARY

Adams, Jacqueline	320917	Miller, Michael	511806
Black, Leslie	813406	Pratt, William	214411
Cook, Marie	511616	Rogers, Ellen	722428
Fisher, Pat	914625	Saunders, Sally	310229
Jackson, Lee	923212	Wilson, Jan	416715
James, Linda	624621	Wyatt, Mark	321326
Lane, Arthur	115702		

10. According to the list, the number of women referred to the laboratory during January was
    A. 4   B. 5   C. 6   D. 7

11. The clinic from which the MOST patients were referred was
    A. Cardiac
    B. Gynecology
    C. Ophthalmology
    D. Pediatrics

12. The YOUNGEST patient referred from any clinic other than Pediatrics was
    A. Leslie Black
    B. Marie Cook
    C. Arthur Lane
    D. Sally Saunders

13. The number of patients whose laboratory tests were performed on or before January 16 was
    A. 7   B. 8   C. 9   D. 10

14. The number of patients referred for laboratory tests who are under age 45 is
    A. 7   B. 8   C. 9   D. 10

15. The OLDEST patient referred to the clinic during January was
    A. Jacqueline Adams
    B. Linda James
    C. Arthur Lane
    D. Jan Wilson

16. The ONLY patient treated in the Orthopedics clinic was
    A. Marie Cook
    B. Pat Fisher
    C. Ellen Rogers
    D. Jan Wilson

17. A woman, age 37 was referred from the Hematology clinic to the laboratory. Her laboratory tests were performed on January 9.
    Her identification number would be
    A. 610937   B. 623709   C. 613790   D. 623790

18. A man was referred for lab tests from the Orthopedics clinic. He is 30 years old and his tests were performed on January 6.
His identification number would be
   A. 413006   B. 510360   C. 513006   D. 513060

18.____

19. A 4-year-old boy was referred from the Pediatrics clinic to have laboratory tests on January 23.
His identification number was
   A. 310422   B. 310423   C. 310433   D. 320403

19.____

KEY (CORRECT ANSWERS)

1.	B	11.	D
2.	B	12.	B
3.	B	13.	A
4.	D	14.	C
5.	D	15.	D
6.	B	16.	A
7.	A	17.	B
8.	D	18.	C
9.	C	19.	B
10.	B		

TEST 4

DIRECTIONS: Each question or incomplete statement is followed by several suggested answers or completions. Select the one that BEST answers the question or completes the statement. *PRINT THE LETTER OF THE CORRECT ANSWER IN THE SPACE AT THE RIGHT.*

Questions 1-10.

DIRECTIONS: Questions 1 through 10 are to be answered on the basis of the information and directions given below.

Assume that you are a Senior Stenographer assigned to the personnel bureau of a city agency. Your supervisor has asked you to classify the employees in your agency into the following five groups:

- A. Employees who are college graduates, who are at least 35 years of age but less than 50, and who have been employed by the City for five years or more;
- B. Employees who have been employed by the City for less than five years, who are not college graduates, and who earn at least $32,500 a year but less than $34,500;
- C. Employees who have been City employees for five years or more, who are at least 21 years of age but less than 35, and who are not college graduates;
- D. Employee who earn at least $34,500 a year but less than $36,000 who are college graduates, and who have been employed by the City for less than five years;
- E. Employees who are not included in any of the foregoing groups.

NOTE: In classifying these employees you are to compute age and period of service as of January 1, 2003. In all cases, it is to be assumed that each employee has been employed continuously in City service. In each question, consider only the information which will assist you in classifying each employee. Any information which is of no assistance in classifying an employee would not be considered.

SAMPLE: Mr. Brown, a 29-year-old veteran, was appointed to his present position of Clerk on June 1, 2000. He has completed two years of college. His present salary is $33,050.

The correct answer to this sample is B, since the employee has been employed by the City for less than five years, is not a college graduate, and earn at least $32,500 a year but less than $34,500.

Questions 1 through 10 contain excerpts from the personnel records of 10 employees in the agency. In the correspondingly numbered space at the right print the capital letter preceding the appropriate group into which you would place each employee.

1. Mr. James has been employed by the City since 1993, when he was graduated from a local college. Now 35 years of age, he earns $36,000 a year.   1.____

2. Mr. Worth began working in City service early in 1999. He was awarded his college degree in 1994, at the age of 21. As a result of a recent promotion, he now earns $34,500 a year.   2.____

2 (#4)

3. Miss Thomas has been a City employee since August 1, 1998. Her salary is $34,500 a year. Miss Thomas, who is 25 years old, has had only three years of high school training.

3.____

4. Mr. Williams has had three promotions since entering City service on January 1, 1991. He was graduated from college with honors in 1974, when he was 20 years of age. His present salary is $37,000 a year.

4.____

5. Miss Jones left college after two years of study to take an appointment to a position in the City service paying $33,300 a year. She began work on March 1, 1997 when she was 19 years of age.

5.____

6. Mr. Smith was graduated from an engineering college with honors in January 1998 and became a City employee three months later. His present salary is $35,810. Mr. Smith was born in 1976.

6.____

7. Miss Earnest was born on May 31, 1979. Her education consisted of four years of high school and one year of business school. She was appointed as a typist in a City agency on June 1, 1997. Her annual salary is $33,500.

7.____

8. Mr. Adams, a 24-year-old clerk, began his City service on July 1, 1999, soon after being discharged from the U.S. Army. A college graduate, his present annual salary is $33,200.

8.____

9. Miss Charles attends college in the evenings, hoping to obtain her degree is 2004, when she will be 30 years of age. She has been a City employee since April 1998, and earns $33,350.

9.____

10. Mr. Dolan was just promoted to his present position after six years of City service. He was graduated from high school in 1982, when he was 18 years of age, but did not go on to college. Mr. Dolan's present salary is $33,500.

10.____

KEY (CORRECT ANSWERS)

1.	A	6.	D
2.	D	7.	C
3.	E	8.	E
4.	A	9.	B
5.	C	10.	E

TEST 5

DIRECTIONS: Questions 1 through 4 each contain five numbers that should be arranged in numerical order. The number with the lowest numerical value should be first and the number with the highest numerical value should be last. Pick that option which indicates the CORRECT order of the numbers.

Examples: A. 9; 18; 14; 15; 27
 B. 9; 14; 15; 18; 27
 C. 14; 15; 18; 27; 9
 D. 9; 14; 15; 27; 18

The correct answer is B, which contains the proper arrangement of the five numbers.

1. A. 20573; 20753; 20738; 20837; 20098
   B. 20098; 20753; 20573; 20738; 20837
   C. 20098; 20573; 20753; 20837; 20738
   D. 20098; 20573; 20738; 20753; 20837

1.____

2. A. 113492; 113429; 111314; 113114; 131413
   B. 111314; 113114; 113429; 113492; 131413
   C. 111314; 113429; 113492; 113114; 131413
   D. 111314; 113114; 131413; 113429; 113492

2.____

3. A. 1029763; 1030421; 1035681; 1036928; 1067391
   B. 1030421; 1029763; 1035681; 1067391; 1036928
   C. 1030421; 1035681; 1036928; 1067391; 1029763
   D. 1029763; 1039421; 1035681; 1067391; 1036928

3.____

4. A. 1112315; 1112326; 1112337; 1112349; 1112306
   B. 1112306; 1112315; 1112337; 1112326; 1112349
   C. 1112306; 1112315; 1112326; 1112337; 1112349
   D. 1112306; 1112326; 1112315; 1112337; 1112349

4.____

KEY (CORRECT ANSWERS)

1. D
2. B
3. A
4. C

TEST 6

DIRECTIONS: The phonetic filing system is a method of filing names in which the alphabet is reduced to key code letters. The six key letters and their equivalents are as follows:

KEY LETTERS	EQUIVALENTS
b	p, f, v
c	s, k, g, j, q, x, z
d	t
l	none
m	n
r	none

A key letter represents itself.
Vowels (a, e, i, o, and u) and the letters w, h, and y are omitted.
For example, the name GILMAN would be represented as follows:
  G is represented by the key letter C.
  I is a vowel and is omitted.
  L is a letter and represents itself.
  M is a key letter and represents itself.
  A is a vowel and is omitted.
  N is represented by the key letter M.

Therefore, the phonetic filing code for the name GILMAN is CLMM.

Answer Questions 1 through 10 based on the information below.

1. The phonetic filing code for the name FITZGERALD would be
   A. BDCCRLD   B. BDCRLD   C. BDZCRLD   D. BTZCRLD

2. The phonetic filing code CLBR may represent any one of the following names EXCEPT
   A. Calprey   B. Flower   C. Glover   D. Silver

3. The phonetic filing code LDM may represent any one of the following names EXCEPT
   A. Halden   B. Hilton   C. Walton   D. Wilson

4. The phonetic filing code for the name RODRIGUEZ would be
   A. RDRC   B. RDRCC   C. RDRCZ   D. RTRCC

5. The phonetic filing code for the name MAXWELL would be
   A. MCLL   B. MCWL   C. MCWLL   D. MXLL

6. The phonetic filing code for the name ANDERSON would be
   A. AMDRCM   B. ENDRSM   C. MDRCM   D. NDERCN

7. The phonetic filing code for the name SAVITSKY would be
   A. CBDCC   B. CBDCY   C. SBDCC   D. SVDCC

2 (#6)

8. The phonetic filing code CMC may represent any one of the following names EXCEPT 8.____
   A. James   B. Jayes   C. Johns   D. Jones

9. The ONLY one of the following names that could be represented by the phonetic filing code CDDDM would be 9.____
   A. Catalano   B. Chesterton   C. Cittadino   D. Cuttlerman

10. The ONLY one of the following names that could be represented by the phonetic filing code LLMCM would be 10.____
    A. Ellington   B. Hallerman   C. Inslerman   D. Willingham

KEY (CORRECT ANSWERS)

1.	A	6.	C
2.	B	7.	A
3.	D	8.	B
4.	B	9.	C
5.	A	10.	D

PREPARING WRITTEN MATERIALS
EXAMINATION SECTION
TEST 1

DIRECTIONS: Each question consists of a sentence which may be classified appropriately under one of the following four categories:
- A. Incorrect because of faulty grammar or sentence structure.
- B. Incorrect because of faulty punctuation.
- C. Incorrect because of faulty spelling or capitalization.
- D. Correct

Examine each sentence carefully. Then, in the space at the right, print the capital letter preceding the option which is the BEST of the four suggested above. All incorrect sentences contain only one type of error. Consider a sentence correct if it contains none of the types of errors mentioned, although there may be other correct ways of expressing the same thought.

1. The fire apparently started in the storeroom, which is usually locked.   1.____
2. On approaching the victim two bruises were noticed by this officer.   2.____
3. The officer, who was there examined the report with great care.   3.____
4. Each employee in the office had a separate desk.   4.____
5. The suggested procedure is similar to the one now in use.   5.____
6. No one was more pleased with the new procedure than the chauffeur.   6.____
7. He tried to pursuade her to change the procedure.   7.____
8. The total of the expenses charged to petty cash were high.   8.____
9. An understanding between him and I was finally reached.   9.____
10. It was at the supervisor's request that the clerk agreed to postpone his vacation.   10.____
11. We do not believe that it is necessary for both he and the clerk to attend the conference.   11.____
12. All employees, who display perseverance, will be given adequate recognition.   12.____
13. He regrets that some of us employees are dissatisfied with our new assignments.   13.____

14. "Do you think that the raise was merited," asked the supervisor? 14.____

15. The new manual of procedure is a valuable supplament to our rules and regulation. 15.____

16. The typist admitted that she had attempted to pursuade the other employees to assist her in her work. 16.____

17. The supervisor asked that all amendments to the regulations be handled by you and I. 17.____

18. They told both he and I that the prisoner had escaped. 18.____

19. Any superior officer, who, disregards the just complaints of his subordinates, is remiss in the performance of his duty. 19.____

20. Only those members of the national organization who resided in the Middle west attended the conference in Chicago. 20.____

21. We told him to give the investigation assignment to whoever was available. 21.____

22. Please do not disappoint and embarass us by not appearing in court. 22.____

23. Despite the efforts of the Supervising mechanic, the elevator could not be started. 23.____

24. The U.S. Weather Bureau, weather record for the accident date was checked. 24.____

KEY (CORRECT ANSWERS)

1.	D		11.	A
2.	A		12.	B
3.	B		13.	D
4.	D		14.	B
5.	D		15.	C
6.	D		16.	C
7.	C		17.	A
8.	A		18.	A
9.	A		19.	B
10.	D		20.	C

21. D
22. C
23. C
24. B

TEST 2

DIRECTIONS: Each question consists of a sentence. Some of the sentences contain errors in English grammar or usage, punctuation, spelling, or capitalization. A sentence does not contain an error simply because it could be written in a different manner. Choose answer:
- A. If the sentence contains an error in English grammar or usage.
- B. if the sentence contains an error in punctuation.
- C. If the sentence contains an error in spelling or capitalization
- D. If the sentence does not contain any errors.

1. The severity of the sentence prescribed by contemporary statutes—including both the former and the revised New York Penal Laws—do not depend on what crime was intended by the offender. 1.____

2. It is generally recognized that two defects in the early law of attempt played a part in the birth of burglary: (1) immunity from prosecution for conduct short of the last act before completion of the crime, and (2) the relatively minor penalty imposed for an attempt (it being a common law misdemeanor) vis-à-vis the completed offense. 2.____

3. The first sentence of the statute is applicable to employees who enter their place of employment, invited guests, and all other persons who have an express or implied license or privilege to enter the premises. 3.____

4. Contemporary criminal codes in the United States generally divide burglary into various degrees, differentiating the categories according to place, time and other attendent circumstances. 4.____

5. The assignment was completed in record time but the payroll for it has not yet been prepaid. 5.____

6. The operator, on the other hand, is willing to learn me how to use the mimeograph. 6.____

7. She is the prettiest of the three sisters. 7.____

8. She doesn't know; if the mail has arrived. 8.____

9. The doorknob of the office door is broke. 9.____

10. Although the department's supply of scratch pads and stationery have diminished considerably, the allotment for our division has not been reduced. 10.____

11. You have not told us whom you wish to designate as your secretary. 11.____

12. Upon reading the minutes of the last meeting, the new proposal was taken up for consideration. 12.____

13. Before beginning the discussion, we locked the door as a precautionery measure. 13._____

14. The supervisor remarked, "Only those clerks, who perform routine work, are permitted to take a rest period." 14._____

15. Not only will this duplicating machine make accurate copies, but it will also produce a quantity of work equal to fifteen transcribing typists. 15._____

16. "Mr. Jones," said the supervisor, "we regret our inability to grant you an extention of your leave of absence." 16._____

17. Although the employees find the work monotonous and fatigueing, they rarely complain. 17._____

18. We completed the tabulation of the receipts on time despite the fact that Miss Smith our fastest operator was absent for over a week. 18._____

19. The reaction of the employees who attended the meeting, as well as the reaction of those who did not attend, indicates clearly that the schedule is satisfactory to everyone concerned. 19._____

20. Of the two employees, the one in our office is the most efficient. 20._____

21. No one can apply or even understand, the new rules and regulations. 21._____

22. A large amount of supplies were stored in the empty office. 22._____

23. If an employee is occassionally asked to work overtime, he should do so willingly. 23._____

24. It is true that the new procedures are difficult to use but, we are certain that you will learn them quickly. 24._____

25. The office manager said that he did not know who would be given a large allotment under the new plan. 25._____

KEY (CORRECT ANSWERS)

1. A
2. D
3. D
4. C
5. C

6. A
7. D
8. B
9. A
10. A

11. D
12. A
13. C
14. B
15. A

16. C
17. C
18. B
19. D
20. A

21. B
22. A
23. C
24. B
25. D

TEST 3

DIRECTIONS: Each of the following sentences may be classified MOST appropriately under one of the following categories:
    A. Faulty because of incorrect grammar
    B. Faulty because of incorrect punctuation
    C. Faulty because of incorrect capitalization
    D. Correct

Examine each sentence carefully. Then, in the space at the right, print the capital letter preceding the option which is the BEST of the four suggested above. All incorrect sentence contain but one type of error. Consider a sentence correct if it contains none of the types of errors mentioned, even though there may be other correct ways of expressing the same thought.

1. The desk, as well as the chairs, were moved out of the office.   1._____

2. The clerk whose production was greatest for the month won a day's vacation as first prize.   2._____

3. Upon entering the room, the employees were found hard at work at their desks.   3._____

4. John Smith our new employee always arrives at work on time.   4._____

5. Punish whoever is guilty of stealing the money.   5._____

6. Intelligent and persistent effort lead to success no matter what the job may be.   6._____

7. The secretary asked, "can you call again at three o'clock?"   7._____

8. He told us, that if the report was not accepted at the next meeting, it would have to be rewritten.   8._____

9. He would not have sent the letter if he had known that it would cause so much excitement.   9._____

10. We all looked forward to him coming to visit us.   10._____

11. If you find that you are unable to complete the assignment please notify me as soon as possible.   11._____

12. Every girl in the office went home on time but me; there was still some work for me to finish.   12._____

13. He wanted to know who the letter was addressed to, Mr. Brown or Mr. Smith.   13._____

14. "Mr. Jones, he said, please answer this letter as soon as possible."   14._____

15. The new clerk had an unusual accent inasmuch as he was born and educated in the south.   15._____

16. Although he is younger than her, he earns a higher salary.   16._____

17. Neither of the two administrators are going to attend the conference being held in Washington, D.C.   17._____

18. Since Miss Smith and Miss Jones have more experience than us, they have been given more responsible duties.   18._____

19. Mr. Shaw the supervisor of the stock room maintains an inventory of stationery and office supplies.   19._____

20. Inasmuch as this matter affects both you and I, we should take joint action.   20._____

21. Who do you think will be able to perform this highly technical work?   21._____

22. Of the two employees, John is considered the most competent.   22._____

23. He is not coming home on tuesday; we expect him next week.   23._____

24. Stenographers, as well as typists must be able to type rapidly and accurately.   24._____

25. Having been placed in the safe we were sure that the money would not be stolen.   25._____

KEY (CORRECT ANSWERS)

1.	A	11.	B
2.	D	12.	D
3.	A	13.	A
4.	B	14.	B
5.	D	15.	C
6.	A	16.	A
7.	C	17.	A
8.	B	18.	A
9.	D	19.	B
10.	A	20.	A

21. D
22. A
23. C
24. B
25. A

TEST 4

DIRECTIONS: Each of the following sentences consist of four sentences lettered A, B, C, and D. One of the sentences in each group contains an error in grammar or punctuation. Indicate the INCORRECT sentence in each group. *PRINT THE LETTER OF THE CORRECT ANSWER IN THE SPACE AT THE RIGHT.*

1. A. Give the message to whoever is on duty.
   B. The teacher who's pupil won first prize presented the award.
   C. Between you and me, I don't expect the program to succeed.
   D. His running to catch the bus caused the accident.

   1.____

2. A. The process, which was patented only last year is already obsolete.
   B. His interest in science (which continues to the present) led him to convert his basement into a laboratory.
   C. He described the book as "verbose, repetitious, and bombastic".
   D. Our new director will need to possess three qualities: vision, patience, and fortitude.

   2.____

3. A. The length of ladder trucks varies considerably.
   B. The probationary fireman reported to the officer to who he was assigned.
   C. The lecturer emphasized the need for we firemen to be punctual.
   D. Neither the officers nor the members of the company knew about the new procedure.

   3.____

4. A. Ham and eggs is the specialty of the house.
   B. He is one of the students who are on probation.
   C. Do you think that either one of us have a chance to be nominated for president of the class?
   D. I assume that either he was to be in charge or you were.

   4.____

5. A. Its a long road that has no turn.
   B. To run is more tiring than to walk.
   C. We have been assigned three new reports: namely, the statistical summary, the narrative summary, and the budgetary summary.
   D. Had the first payment been made in January, the second would be due in April.

   5.____

6. A. Each employer has his own responsibilities.
   B. If a person speaks correctly, they make a good impression.
   C. Every one of the operators has had her vacation.
   D. Has anybody filed his report?

   6.____

7. A. The manager, with all his salesmen, was obliged to go.
   B. Who besides them is to sign the agreement?
   C. One report without the others is incomplete.
   D. Several clerks, as well as the proprietor, was injured.

   7.____

8. A. A suspension of these activities is expected.
    B. The machine is economical because first cost and upkeep are low.
    C. A knowledge of stenography and filing are required for this position.
    D. The condition in which the goods were received shows that the packing was not done properly.

9. A. There seems to be a great many reasons for disagreement.
    B. It does not seem possible that they could have failed.
    C. Have there always been too few applicants for these positions?
    D. There is no excuse for these errors.

10. A. We shall be pleased to answer your question.
    B. Shall we plan the meeting for Saturday?
    C. I will call you promptly at seven.
    D. Can I borrow your book after you have read it?

11. A. You are as capable as I.
    B. Everyone is willing to sign but him and me.
    C. As for he and his assistant, I cannot praise them too highly.
    D. Between you and me, I think he will be dismissed.

12. A. Our competitors bid above us last week.
    B. The survey which was began last year has not yet been completed.
    C. The operators had shown that they understood their instructions.
    D. We have never ridden over worse roads.

13. A. Who did they say was responsible?
    B. Whom did you suspect?
    C. Who do you suppose it was?
    D. Whom do you mean?

14. A. Of the two propositions, this is the worse.
    B. Which report do you consider the best—the one in January or the one in July?
    C. I believe this is the most practicable of the many plans submitted.
    D. He is the youngest employee in the organization.

15. A. The firm had but three orders last week.
    B. That doesn't really seem possible.
    C. After twenty years scarcely none of the old business remains.
    D. Has he done nothing about it?

KEY (CORRECT ANSWERS)

1.	B	6.	B	11.	C
2.	A	7.	D	12.	B
3.	C	8.	C	13.	A
4.	C	9.	A	14.	B
5.	A	10.	D	15.	C

PREPARING WRITTEN MATERIAL

PARAGRAPH REARRANGEMENT
COMMENTARY

The sentences that follow are in scrambled order. You are to rearrange them in proper order and indicate the letter choice containing the correct answer at the space at the right.

Each group of sentences in this section is actually a paragraph presented in scrambled order. Each sentence in the group has a place in that paragraph; no sentence is to be left out. You are to read each group of sentences and decide upon the best order in which to put the sentences so as to form a well-organized paragraph.

The questions in this section measure the ability to solve a problem when all the facts relevant to its solution are not given.

More specifically, certain positions of responsibility and authority require the employee to discover connection between events sometimes, apparently, unrelated. In order to do this, the employee will find it necessary to correctly infer that unspecified events have probably occurred or are likely to occur. This ability becomes especially important when action must be taken on incomplete information.

Accordingly, these questions require competitors to choose among several suggested alternatives, each of which presents a different sequential arrangement of the events. Competitors must choose the MOST logical of the suggested sequences.

In order to do so, they may be required to draw on general knowledge to infer missing concepts or events that are essential to sequencing the given events. Competitors should be careful to infer only what is essential to the sequence. The plausibility of the wrong alternatives will always require the inclusion of unlikely events or of additional chains of events which are NOT essential to sequencing the given events.

It's very important to remember that you are looking for the best of the four possible choices, and that the best choice of all may not even be one of the answers you're given to choose from.

There is no one right way to solve these problems. Many people have found it helpful to first write out the order of the sentences, as they would have arranged them, on their scrap paper before looking at the possible answers. If their optimum answer is there, this can save them some time. If it isn't, this method can still give insight into solving the problem. Others find it most helpful to just go through each of the possible choices, contrasting each as they go along. You should use whatever method feels comfortable and works for you.

While most of these types of questions are not that difficult, we've added a higher percentage of the difficult type, just to give you more practice. Usually there are only one or two questions on this section that contain such subtle distinctions that you're unable to answer confidently. And you then may find yourself stuck deciding between two possible choices, neither of which you're sure about.

———

EXAMINATION SECTION
TEST 1

DIRECTIONS: Each question consists of several sentences which can be arranged in a logical sequence. For each question, select the choice which places the numbered sentences in the MOST logical sequence. *PRINT THE LETTER OF THE CORRECT ANSWER IN THE SPACE AT THE RIGHT.*

1. I. A body was found in the woods.
   II. A man proclaimed innocence.
   III. The owner of a gun was located.
   IV. A gun was traced.
   V. The owner of a gun was questioned.
   The CORRECT answer is:
   A. IV, III, V, II, I
   B. II, I, IV, III, V
   C. I, IV, III, V, II
   D. I, III, V, II, IV
   E. I, II, IV, III, V

   1.____

2. I. A man is in a hunting accident.
   II. A man fell down a flight of steps.
   III. A man lost his vision in one eye,
   IV. A man broke his leg.
   V. A man had to walk with a cane.
   The CORRECT answer is:
   A. II, IV, V, I, III
   B. IV, V, I, III, II
   C. III, I, IV, V, II
   D. I, III, V, II, IV
   E. I, III, II, IV, V

   2.____

3. I. A man is offered a new job.
   II. A woman is offered a new job.
   III. A man works as a waiter.
   IV. A woman works as a waitress.
   V. A woman gives notice.
   The CORRECT answer is:
   A. IV, II, V, III, I
   B. IV, II, V, I, III
   C. II, IV, V, III, I
   D. III, I, IV, II, V
   E. IV, III, II, V, I

   3.____

4. I. A train let the station late.
   II. A man was late for work.
   III. A man lost his job.
   IV. Many people complained because the train was late.
   V. There was a traffic jam.
   The CORRECT answer is:
   A. V, II, I, IV, III
   B. V, I, IV, II, III
   C. V, I, II, IV, III
   D. I, V, IV, II, III
   E. II, I, IV, V, III

   4.____

5.
  I. The burden of proof as to each issue is determined before trial and remains upon the same party throughout the trial.
  II. The jury is at liberty to believe one witness' testimony as against a number of contradictory witnesses.
  III. In a civil case, the party bearing the burden of proof is required to prove his contention by a fair preponderance of the evidence.
  IV. However, it must be noted that a fair preponderance of evidence does not necessarily mean a greater number of witnesses.
  V. The burden of proof is the burden which rests upon one of the parties to an action to persuade the trier of the facts, generally the jury, that a proposition he asserts is true.
  VI. If the evidence is equally balanced, or if it leaves the jury in such doubt as to be unable to decide the controversy either way, judgment must be given against the party upon whom the burden of proof rests.
  The CORRECT answer is:
   A. III. II, V, IV, I, VI   B. I, II, VI, V, III, IV   C. III, IV, V, I, II, VI
   D. V, I, III, VI, IV, II   E. I, V, III, VI, IV, II

6.
  I. If a parent is without assets and is unemployed, he cannot be convicted of the crime of non-support of a child.
  II. The term *sufficient ability* has been held to mean sufficient financial ability.
  III. It does not matter if his unemployment is by choice or unavoidable circumstances.
  IV. If he fails to take any steps at all, he may be liable to prosecution for endangering the welfare of a child.
  V. Under the penal law, a parent is responsible for the support of his minor child only if the parent is of *sufficient ability*.
  VI. An indigent parent may meet his obligation by borrowing money or by seeking aid under the provisions of the Social Welfare Law.
  The CORRECT answer is:
   A. VI, I, V, III, II, IV   B. I, III, V, II, IV, VI   C. V, II, I, III, VI, IV
   D. I, VI, IV, V, II, III   E. II, V, I, III, VI, IV

7.
  I. Consider, for example, the case of a rabble rouser who urges a group of twenty people to go out and break the windows of a nearby factory.
  II. Therefore, the law fills the indicated gap with the crime of *inciting to riot*.
  III. A person is considered guilty of inciting to riot when he urges ten or more persons to engage in tumultuous and violent conduct of a kind likely to create public alarm.
  IV. However, if he has not obtained the cooperation of at least four people, he cannot be charged with unlawful assembly.
  V. The charge of inciting to riot was added to the law to cover types of conduct which cannot be classified as either the crime of *riot* or the crime of *unlawful assembly*.
  VI. If he acquires the acquiescence of at least four of them, he is guilty of unlawful assembly even if the project does not materialize.
  The CORRECT answer is:
   A. III, V, I, VI, IV, II   B. V, I, IV, VI, II, III   C. III, IV, I, V, II, VI
   D. V, I, IV, VI, III, II   E. V, III, I, VI, IV, II

8. I. If, however, the rebuttal evidence presents an issue of credibility, it is for the jury to determine whether the presumption has, in fact, been destroyed.
    II. Once sufficient evidence to the contrary is introduced, the presumption disappears from the trial.
    III. The effect of a presumption is to place the burden upon the adversary to come forward with evidence to rebut the presumption.
    IV. When a presumption is overcome and ceases to exist in the case, the fact or facts which gave rise to the presumption still remain.
    V. Whether a presumption has been overcome is ordinarily a question for the court.
    VI. Such information may furnish a basis for a logical inference.
    The CORRECT answer is:
    A. IV, VI, II, V, I, III
    B. III, II, V, I, IV, VI
    C. V, III, VI, IV, II, I
    D. V, IV, I, II, VI, III
    E. II, III, V, I, IV, VI

8.____

9. I. An executive may answer a letter by writing his reply on the face of the letter itself instead of having a return letter typed.
    II. This procedure is efficient because it saves the executive's time, the typist's time, and saves office file space.
    III. Copying machines are used in small offices as well as large offices to save time and money in making brief replies to business letters.
    IV. A copy is made on a copying machine to go into the company files, while the original is mailed back to the sender.
    The CORRECT answer is:
    A. I, II, IV, III
    B. I, IV, II, III
    C. III, I, IV, II
    D. III, IV, II, I

9.____

10. I. Most organizations favor one of the types but always include the others to a lesser degree.
    II. However, we can detect a definite trend toward greater use of symbolic control.
    III. We suggest that our local police agencies are today primarily utilizing material control.
    IV. Control can be classified into three types: physical, material, and symbolic.
    The CORRECT answer is:
    A. IV, II, III, I
    B. II, I, IV, III
    C. III, IV, II, I
    D. IV, I, III, II

10.____

11. I. Project residents had first claim to this use, followed by surrounding neighborhood children.
    II. By contrast, recreation space within the project's interior was found to be used more often by both groups.
    III. Studies of the use of project grounds in many cities showed grounds left open for public use were neglected and unused, both by residents and by members of the surrounding community.
    IV. Project residents had clearly laid claim to the play spaces, setting up and enforcing unwritten rules for use.
    V. Each group, by experience, found their activities easily disrupted by other groups, and their claim to the use of space for recreation difficult to enforce.

11.____

The CORRECT answer is:
A. IV, V, I, II, III
B. V, II, IV, III, I
C. I, IV, III, II, V
D. III, V, II, IV, I

12. I. They do not consider the problems correctable within the existing subsidy formula and social policy of accepting all eligible applicants regardless of social behavior.
    II. A recent survey, however, indicated that tenants believe these problems correctable by local housing authorities and management within the existing financial formula.
    III. Many of the problems and complaints concerning public housing management and design have created resentment between the tenant and the landlord.
    IV. This same survey indicated that administrators and managers do not agree with the tenants.
    The CORRECT answer is:
    A. II, I, III, IV   B. I, III, IV, II   C. III, II, IV, I   D. IV, II, I, III

13. I. In single-family residences, there is usually enough distance between tenants to prevent occupants from annoying one another.
    II. For example, a certain small percentage of tenant families has one or more members addicted to alcohol.
    III. While managers believe in the right of individuals to live as they choose, the manager becomes concerned when the pattern of living jeopardizes others' rights.
    IV. Still others turn night into day, staging lusty entertainments which carry on into the hours when most tenants are trying to sleep.
    V. In apartment buildings, however, tenants live so closely together that any misbehavior can result in unpleasant living conditions.
    VI. Other families engage in violent argument.
    The CORRECT answer is:
    A. III, II, V, IV, VI, I
    B. I, V, II, VI, IV, III
    C. II, V, IV, I, III, VI
    D. IV, II, V, VI, III, I

14. I. Congress made the commitment explicit in the Housing Act of 194, establishing as a national goal the realization of a *decent home and suitable environment for every American family*.
    II. The result has been that the goal of decent home and suitable environment is still as far distant as ever for the disadvantaged urban family.
    III. In spite of this action by Congress, federal housing programs have continued to be fragmented and grossly underfunded.
    IV. The passage of the National Housing Act signaled a few federal commitment to provide housing for the nation's citizens.
    The CORRECT answer is:
    A. I, IV, III, II   B. IV, I, III, II   C. IV, I, II, III   D. II, IV, I, III

15. I. The greater expense does not necessarily involve *exploitation*, but it is often perceived as exploitative and unfair by those who are aware of the price differences involved, but unaware of operating costs.
II. Ghetto residents believe they are *exploited* by local merchants, and evidence substantiates some of these beliefs.
III. However, stores in low-income areas were more likely to be small independents, which could not achieve the economies available to supermarket chains and were, therefore, more likely to charge higher prices, and the customers were more likely to buy smaller-sized packages which are more expensive per unit of measure.
IV. A study conducted in one city showed that distinctly higher prices were charged for goods sold in ghetto stores in other areas.
The CORRECT answer is:
   A. IV, II, I, III   B. IV, I, III, II   C. II, IV, III, I   D. II, III, IV, I

15.____

KEY (CORRECT ANSWERS)

1.	C	6.	C	11.	D
2.	E	7.	A	12.	C
3.	B	8.	B	13.	B
4.	B	9.	C	14.	B
5.	D	10.	D	15.	C

PHILOSOPHY, PRINCIPLES, PRACTICES, AND TECHNICS
OF
SUPERVISION, ADMINISTRATION, MANAGEMENT, AND ORGANIZATION

TABLE OF CONTENTS

	Page
MEANING OF SUPERVISION	1
THE OLD AND THE NEW SUPERVISION	1
THE EIGHT (8) BASIC PRINCIPLES OF THE NEW SUPERVISION	1
I. Principle of Responsibility	1
II. Principle of Authority	2
III. Principle of Self-Growth	2
IV. Principle of Individual Worth	2
V. Principle of Creative Leadership	2
VI. Principle of Success and Failure	2
VII. Principle of Science	3
VIII. Principle of Cooperation	3
WHAT IS ADMINISTRATION?	3
I. Practices Commonly Classed as "Supervisory"	3
II. Practices Commonly Classed as "Administrative"	3
III. Practices Commonly Classed as Both "Supervisory" and "Administrative"	4
RESPONSIBILITIES OF THE SUPERVISOR	4
COMPETENCIES OF THE SUPERVISOR	4
THE PROFESSIONAL SUPERVISOR-EMPLOYEE RELATIONSHIP	4
MINI-TEXT IN SUPERVISION, ADMINISTRATION, MANAGEMENT, AND ORGANIZATION	5
I. Brief Highlights	5
A. Levels of Management	6
B. What the Supervisor Must Learn	6
C. A Definition of Supervision	6
D. Elements of the Team Concept	6
E. Principles of Organization	6
F. The Four Important Parts of Every Job	7
G. Principles of Delegation	7
H. Principles of Effective Communications	7
I. Principles of Work Improvement	7
J. Areas of Job Improvement	7
K. Seven Key Points in Making Improvements	8

	L.	Corrective Techniques for Job Improvement	8
	M.	A Planning Checklist	8
	N.	Five Characteristics of Good Directions	9
	O.	Types of Directions	9
	P.	Controls	9
	Q.	Orienting the New Employee	9
	R.	Checklist for Orienting New Employees	9
	S.	Principles of Learning	10
	T.	Causes of Poor Performance	10
	U.	Four Major Steps in On-the-Job Instructions	10
	V.	Employees Want Five Things	10
	W.	Some Don'ts in Regard to Praise	11
	X.	How to Gain Your Workers' Confidence	11
	Y.	Sources of Employee Problems	11
	Z.	The Supervisor's Key to Discipline	11
	AA.	Five Important Processes of Management	12
	BB.	When the Supervisor Fails to Plan	12
	CC.	Fourteen General Principles of Management	12
	DD.	Change	12
II.	Brief Topical Summaries		13
	A.	Who/What is the Supervisor?	13
	B.	The Sociology of Work	13
	C.	Principles and Practices of Supervision	14
	D.	Dynamic Leadership	14
	E.	Processes for Solving Problems	15
	F.	Training for Results	15
	G.	Health, Safety, and Accident Prevention	16
	H.	Equal Employment Opportunity	16
	I.	Improving Communications	16
	J.	Self-Development	17
	K.	Teaching and Training	17
		1. The Teaching Process	17
		a. Preparation	17
		b. Presentation	18
		c. Summary	18
		d. Application	18
		e. Evaluation	18
		2. Teaching Methods	18
		a. Lecture	18
		b. Discussion	18
		c. Demonstration	19
		d. Performance	19
		e. Which Method to Use	19

PHILOSOPHY, PRINCIPLES, PRACTICES, AND TECHNICS
OF
SUPERVISION, ADMINISTRATION, MANAGEMENT, AND ORGANIZATION

MEANING OF SUPERVISION

The extension of the democratic philosophy has been accompanied by an extension in the scope of supervision. Modern leaders and supervisors no longer think of supervision in the narrow sense of being confined chiefly to visiting employees, supplying materials, or rating the staff. They regard supervision as being intimately related to all the concerned agencies of society, they speak of the supervisor's function in terms of "growth," rather than the "improvement" of employees.

This modern concept of supervision may be defined as follows: Supervision is leadership and the development of leadership within groups which are cooperatively engaged in inspection, research, training, guidance, and evaluation.

THE OLD AND THE NEW SUPERVISION

TRADITIONAL
1. Inspection
2. Focused on the employee
3. Visitation
4. Random and haphazard
5. Imposed and authoritarian
6. One person usually

MODERN
1. Study and analysis
2. Focused on aims, materials, methods, supervisors, employees, environment
3. Demonstrations, intervisitation, workshops, directed reading, bulletins, etc.
4. Definitely organized and planned (scientific)
5. Cooperative and democratic
6. Many persons involved (creative)

THE EIGHT (8) BASIC PRINCIPLES OF THE NEW SUPERVISION

I. Principle of Responsibility
   Authority to act and responsibility for acting must be joined.
   A. If you give responsibility, give authority.
   B. Define employee duties clearly.
   C. Protect employees from criticism by others.
   D. Recognize the rights as well as obligations of employees.
   E. Achieve the aims of a democratic society insofar as it is possible within the area of your work.
   F. Establish a situation favorable to training and learning.
   G. Accept ultimate responsibility for everything done in your section, unit, office, division, department.
   H. Good administration and good supervision are inseparable.

II. Principle of Authority
The success of the supervisor is measured by the extent to which the power of authority is not used.
   A. Exercise simplicity and informality in supervision
   B. Use the simplest machinery of supervision
   C. If it is good for the organization as a whole, it is probably justified.
   D. Seldom be arbitrary or authoritative.
   E. Do not base your work on the power of position or of personality.
   F. Permit and encourage the free expression of opinions.

III. Principle of Self-Growth
The success of the supervisor is measured by the extent to which, and the speed with which, he is no longer needed.
   A. Base criticism on principles, not on specifics.
   B. Point out higher activities to employees.
   C. Train for self-thinking by employees to meet new situations.
   D. Stimulate initiative, self-reliance, and individual responsibility
   E. Concentrate on stimulating the growth of employees rather than on removing defects.

IV. Principle of Individual Worth
Respect for the individual is a paramount consideration in supervision.
   A. Be human and sympathetic in dealing with employees.
   B. Don't nag about things to be done.
   C. Recognize the individual differences among employees and seek opportunities to permit best expression of each personality.

V. Principle of Creative Leadership
The best supervision is that which is not apparent to the employee.
   A. Stimulate, don't drive employees to creative action.
   B. Emphasize doing good things.
   C. Encourage employees to do what they do best.
   D. Do not be too greatly concerned with details of subject or method.
   E. Do not be concerned exclusively with immediate problems and activities.
   F. Reveal higher activities and make them both desired and maximally possible.
   G. Determine procedures in the light of each situation but see that these are derived from a sound basic philosophy.
   H. Aid, inspire, and lead so as to liberate the creative spirit latent in all good employees.

VI. Principle of Success and Failure
There are no unsuccessful employees, only unsuccessful supervisors who have failed to give proper leadership.
   A. Adapt suggestions to the capacities, attitudes, and prejudices of employees.
   B. Be gradual, be progressive, be persistent.
   C. Help the employee find the general principle; have the employee apply his own problem to the general principle.
   D. Give adequate appreciation for good work and honest effort.
   E. Anticipate employee difficulties and help to prevent them.
   F. Encourage employees to do the desirable things they will do anyway.
   G. Judge your supervision by the results it secures.

VII. Principle of Science
Successful supervision is scientific, objective, and experimental. It is based on facts, not on prejudices.
  A. Be cumulative in results.
  B. Never divorce your suggestions from the goals of training.
  C. Don't be impatient of results.
  D. Keep all matters on a professional, not a personal, level.
  E. Do not be concerned exclusively with immediate problems and activities.
  F. Use objective means of determining achievement and rating where possible.

VIII. Principle of Cooperation
Supervision is a cooperative enterprise between supervisor and employee.
  A. Begin with conditions as they are.
  B. Ask opinions of all involved when formulating policies.
  C. Organization is as good as its weakest link.
  D. Let employees help to determine policies and department programs.
  E. Be approachable and accessible—physically and mentally.
  F. Develop pleasant social relationships.

WHAT IS ADMINISTRATION

Administration is concerned with providing the environment, the material facilities, and the operational procedures that will promote the maximum growth and development of supervisors and employees. (Organization is an aspect and a concomitant of administration.)

There is no sharp line of demarcation between supervision and administration; these functions are intimately interrelated and, often, overlapping. They are complementary activities.

I. Practices Commonly Classed as "Supervisory"
  A. Conducting employees' conferences
  B. Visiting sections, units, offices, divisions, departments
  C. Arranging for demonstrations
  D. Examining plans
  E. Suggesting professional reading
  F. Interpreting bulletins
  G. Recommending in-service training courses
  H. Encouraging experimentation
  I. Appraising employee morale
  J. Providing for intervisitation

II. Practices Commonly Classified as "Administrative"
  A. Management of the office
  B. Arrangement of schedules for extra duties
  C. Assignment of rooms or areas
  D. Distribution of supplies
  E. Keeping records and reports
  F. Care of audio-visual materials
  G. Keeping inventory records
  H. Checking record cards and books

    I.   Programming special activities
    J.   Checking on the attendance and punctuality of employees

III.   Practices Commonly Classified as Both "Supervisory" and "Administrative"
    A.   Program construction
    B.   Testing or evaluating outcomes
    C.   Personnel accounting
    D.   Ordering instructional materials

RESPONSIBILITIES OF THE SUPERVISOR

A person employed in a supervisory capacity must constantly be able to improve his own efficiency and ability. He represent the employer to the employees and only continuous self-examination can make him a capable supervisor.

Leadership and training are the supervisor's responsibility. An efficient working unit is one in which the employees work with the supervisor. It is his job to bring out the best in his employees. He must always be relaxed, courteous, and calm in his association with his employees. Their feelings are important, and a harsh attitude does not develop the most efficient employees.

COMPETENCES OF THE SUPERVISOR

    I.   Complete knowledge of the duties and responsibilities of his position.
    II.   To be able to organize a job, plan ahead, and carry through.
    III. To have self-confidence and initiative.
    IV. To be able to handle the unexpected situation and make quick decisions.
    V.   To be able to properly train subordinates in the positions they are best suited for.
    VI. To be able to keep good human relations among his subordinates.
    VII. To be able to keep good human relations between his subordinates and himself and to earn their respect and trust.

THE PROFESSIONAL SUPERVISOR-EMPLOYEE RELATIONSHIP

There are two kinds of efficiency: one kind is only apparent and is produced in organizations through the exercise of mere discipline; this is but a simulation of the second, or true, efficiency which springs from spontaneous cooperation. If you are a manager, no matter how great or small your responsibility, it is your job, in the final analysis, to create and develop this involuntary cooperation among the people whom you supervise. For, no matter how powerful a combination of money, machines, and materials a company may have, this is a dead and sterile thing without a team of willing, thinking, and articulate people to guide it.

The following 21 points are presented as indicative of the exemplary basic relationship that should exist between supervisor and employee:

1. Each person wants to be liked and respected by his fellow employee and wants to be treated with consideration and respect by his superior.
2. The most competent employee will make an error. However, in a unit where good relations exist between the supervisor and his employees, tenseness and fear do not exist. Thus, errors are not hidden or covered up, and the efficiency of a unit is not impaired.

3. Subordinates resent rules, regulations, or orders that are unreasonable or unexplained.
4. Subordinates are quick to resent unfairness, harshness, injustices, and favoritism.
5. An employee will accept responsibility if he knows that he will be complimented for a job well done, and not too harshly chastised for failure; that his supervisor will check the cause of the failure, and, if it was the supervisor's fault, he will assume the blame therefore. If it was the employee's fault, his supervisor will explain the correct method or means of handling the responsibility.
6. An employee wants to receive credit for a suggestion he has made, that is used. If a suggestion cannot be used, the employee is entitled to an explanation. The supervisor should not say "no" and close the subject.
7. Fear and worry slow up a worker's ability. Poor working environment can impair his physical and mental health. A good supervisor avoids forceful methods, threats, and arguments to get a job done.
8. A forceful supervisor is able to train his employees individually and as a team, and is able to motivate them in the proper channels.
9. A mature supervisor is able to properly evaluate his subordinates and to keep them happy and satisfied.
10. A sensitive supervisor will never patronize his subordinates.
11. A worthy supervisor will respect his employees' confidences.
12. Definite and clear-cut responsibilities should be assigned to each executive.
13. Responsibility should always be coupled with corresponding authority.
14. No change should be made in the scope or responsibilities of a position without a definite understanding to that effect on the part of all persons concerned.
15. No executive or employee, occupying a single position in the organization, should be subject to definite orders from more than one source.
16. Orders should never be given to subordinates over the head of a responsible executive. Rather than do this, the officer in question should be supplanted.
17. Criticisms of subordinates should, whoever possible, be made privately, and in no case should a subordinate be criticized in the presence of executives or employees of equal or lower rank.
18. No dispute or difference between executives or employees as to authority or responsibilities should be considered too trivial for prompt and careful adjudication.
19. Promotions, wage changes, and disciplinary action should always be approved by the executive immediately superior to the one directly responsible.
20. No executive or employee should ever be required, or expected, to be at the same time an assistant to, and critic of, another.
21. Any executive whose work is subject to regular inspection should, wherever practicable, be given the assistance and facilities necessary to enable him to maintain an independent check of the quality of his work.

MINI-TEXT IN SUPERVISION, ADMINISTRATION, MANAGEMENT, AND ORGANIZATION

I. Brief Highlights

Listed concisely and sequentially are major headings and important data in the field for quick recall and review.

A. Levels of Management
Any organization of some size has several levels of management. In terms of a ladder, the levels are:

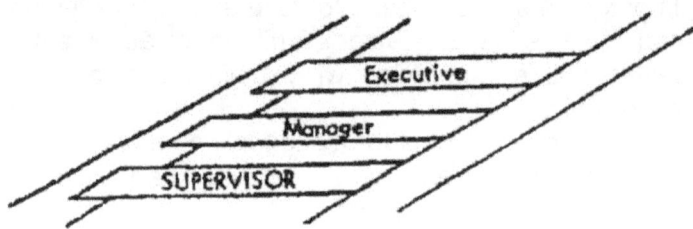

The first level is very important because it is the beginning point of management leadership.

B. What the Supervisor Must Learn
A supervisor must learn to:
1. Deal with people and their differences
2. Get the job done through people
3. Recognize the problems when they exist
4. Overcome obstacles to good performance
5. Evaluate the performance of people
6. Check his own performance in terms of accomplishment

C. A Definition of Supervisor
The term supervisor means any individual having authority, in the interests of the employer, to hire, transfer, suspend, lay-off, recall, promote, discharge, assign, reward, or discipline other employees or responsibility to direct them, or to adjust their grievances, or effectively to recommend such action, if, in connection with the foregoing, exercise of such authority is not of a merely routine or clerical nature but requires the use of independent judgment.

D. Elements of the Team Concept
What is involved in teamwork? The component parts are:
1. Members
2. A leader
3. Goals
4. Plans
5. Cooperation
6. Spirit

E. Principles of Organization
1. A team member must know what his job is.
2. Be sure that the nature and scope of a job are understood.
3. Authority and responsibility should be carefully spelled out.
4. A supervisor should be permitted to make the maximum number of decisions affecting his employees.
5. Employees should report to only one supervisor.
6. A supervisor should direct only as many employees as he can handle effectively.
7. An organization plan should be flexible.

8. Inspection and performance of work should be separate.
9. Organizational problems should receive immediate attention.
10. Assign work in line with ability and experience.

F. The Four Important Parts of Every Job
1. Inherent in every job is the *accountability* for results.
2. A second set of factors in every job is *responsibilities*.
3. Along with duties and responsibilities one must have the *authority* to act within certain limits without obtaining permission to proceed.
4. No job exists in a vacuum. The supervisor is surrounded by key *relationships*.

G. Principles of Delegation
Where work is delegated for the first time, the supervisor should think in terms of these questions:
1. Who is best qualified to do this?
2. Can an employee improve his abilities by doing this?
3. How long should an employee spend on this?
4. Are there any special problems for which he will need guidance?
5. How broad a delegation can I make?

H. Principles of Effective Communications
1. Determine the media.
2. To whom directed?
3. Identification and source authority.
4. Is communication understood?

I. Principles of Work Improvement
1. Most people usually do only the work which is assigned to them.
2. Workers are likely to fit assigned work into the time available to perform it.
3. A good workload usually stimulates output.
4. People usually do their best work when they know that results will be reviewed or inspected.
5. Employees usually feel that someone else is responsible for conditions of work, workplace layout, job methods, type of tools/equipment, and other such factors.
6. Employees are usually defensive about their job security.
7. Employees have natural resistance to change.
8. Employees can support or destroy a supervisor.
9. A supervisor usually earns the respect of his people through his personal example of diligence and efficiency.

J. Areas of Job Improvement
The areas of job improvement are quite numerous, but the most common ones which a supervisor can identify and utilize are:
1. Departmental layout
2. Flow of work
3. Workplace layout
4. Utilization of manpower
5. Work methods
6. Materials handling

7. Utilization
8. Motion economy

K. Seven Key Points in Making Improvements
1. Select the job to be improved
2. Study how it is being done now
3. Question the present method
4. Determine actions to be taken
5. Chart proposed method
6. Get approval and apply
7. Solicit worker participation

l. Corrective Techniques of Job Improvement
Specific Problems
1. Size of workload
2. Inability to meet schedules
3. Strain and fatigue
4. Improper use of men and skills
5. Waste, poor quality, unsafe conditions
6. Bottleneck conditions that hinder output
7. Poor utilization of equipment and machine
8. Efficiency and productivity of labor

General Improvement
1. Departmental layout
2. Flow of work
3. Work plan layout
4. Utilization of manpower
5. Work methods
6. Materials handling
7. Utilization of equipment
8. Motion economy

Corrective Techniques
1. Study with scale model
2. Flow chart study
3. Motion analysis
4. Comparison of units produced to standard allowance
5. Methods analysis
6. Flow chart and equipment study
7. Down time vs. running time
8. Motion analysis

M. A Planning Checklist
1. Objectives
2. Controls
3. Delegations
4. Communications
5. Resources
6. Manpower

7. Equipment
8. Supplies and materials
9. Utilization of time
10. Safety
11. Money
12. Work
13. Timing of improvements

N. Five Characteristics of Good Directions
In order to get results, directions must be:
1. Possible of accomplishment
2. Agreeable with worker interests
3. Related to mission
4. Planned and complete
5. Unmistakably clear

O. Types of Directions
1. Demands or direct orders
2. Requests
3. Suggestion or implication
4. volunteering

P. Controls
A typical listing of the overall areas in which the supervisor should establish controls might be:
1. Manpower
2. Materials
3. Quality of work
4. Quantity of work
5. Time
6. Space
7. Money
8. Methods

Q. Orienting the New Employee
1. Prepare for him
2. Welcome the new employee
3. Orientation for the job
4. Follow-up

R. Checklist for Orienting New Employees   Yes   No
1. Do you appreciate the feelings of new employees
   when they first report for work?   ___   ___
2. Are you aware of the fact that the new employee must
   make a big adjustment to his job?   ___   ___
3. Have you given him good reasons for liking the job and
   the organization?   ___   ___
4. Have you prepared for his first day on the job?   ___   ___
5. Did you welcome him cordially and make him feel needed? ___ ___

		Yes	No
6.	Did you establish rapport with him so that he feels free to talk and discuss matters with you?	___	___
7.	Did you explain his job to him and his relationship to you?	___	___
8.	Does he know that his work will be evaluated periodically on a basis that is fair and objective?	___	___
9.	Did you introduce him to his fellow workers in such a way that they are likely to accept him?	___	___
10.	Does he know what employee benefits he will receive?	___	___
11.	Does he understand the importance of being on the job and what to do if he must leave his duty station?	___	___
12.	Has he been impressed with the importance of accident prevention and safe practice?	___	___
13.	Does he generally know his way around the department?	___	___
14.	Is he under the guidance of a sponsor who will teach the right way of doing things?	___	___
15.	Do you plan to follow-up so that he will continue to adjust successfully to his job?	___	___

S. Principles of Learning
   1. Motivation
   2. Demonstration or explanation
   3. Practice

T. Causes of Poor Performance
   1. Improper training for job
   2. Wrong tools
   3. Inadequate directions
   4. Lack of supervisory follow-up
   5. Poor communications
   6. Lack of standards of performance
   7. Wrong work habits
   8. Low morale
   9. Other

U. Four Major Steps in On-The-Job Instruction
   1. Prepare the worker
   2. Present the operation
   3. Tryout performance
   4. Follow-up

V. Employees Want Five Things
   1. Security
   2. Opportunity
   3. Recognition
   4. Inclusion
   5. Expression

W. Some Don'ts in Regard to Praise
1. Don't praise a person for something he hasn't done.
2. Don't praise a person unless you can be sincere.
3. Don't be sparing in praise just because your superior withholds it from you.
4. Don't let too much time elapse between good performance and recognition of it

X. How to Gain Your Workers' Confidence
Methods of developing confidence include such things as:
1. Knowing the interests, habits, hobbies of employees
2. Admitting your own inadequacies
3. Sharing and telling of confidence in others
4. Supporting people when they are in trouble
5. Delegating matters that can be well handled
6. Being frank and straightforward about problems and working conditions
7. Encouraging others to bring their problems to you
8. Taking action on problems which impede worker progress

Y. Sources of Employee Problems
On-the-job causes might be such things as:
1. A feeling that favoritism is exercised in assignments
2. Assignment of overtime
3. An undue amount of supervision
4. Changing methods or systems
5. Stealing of ideas or trade secrets
6. Lack of interest in job
7. Threat of reduction in force
8. Ignorance or lack of communications
9. Poor equipment
10. Lack of knowing how supervisor feels toward employee
11. Shift assignments

Off-the-job problems might have to do with:
1. Health
2. Finances
3. Housing
4. Family

Z. The Supervisor's Key to Discipline
There are several key points about discipline which the supervisor should keep in mind:
1. Job discipline is one of the disciplines of life and is directed by the supervisor.
2. It is more important to correct an employee fault than to fix blame for it.
3. Employee performance is affected by problems both on the job and off.
4. Sudden or abrupt changes in behavior can be indications of important employee problems.
5. Problems should be dealt with as soon as possible after they are identified.
6. The attitude of the supervisor may have more to do with solving problems than the techniques of problem solving.
7. Correction of employee behavior should be resorted to only after the supervisor is sure that training or counseling will not be helpful.

8. Be sure to document your disciplinary actions.
9. Make sure that you are disciplining on the basis of facts rather than personal feelings.
10. Take each disciplinary step in order, being careful not to make snap judgments, or decisions based on impatience.

AA. Five Important Processes of Management
1. Planning
2. Organizing
3. Scheduling
4. Controlling
5. Motivating

BB. When the Supervisor Fails to Plan
1. Supervisor creates impression of not knowing his job
2. May lead to excessive overtime
3. Job runs itself—supervisor lacks control
4. Deadlines and appointments missed
5. Parts of the work go undone
6. Work interrupted by emergencies
7. Sets a bad example
8. Uneven workload creates peaks and valleys
9. Too much time on minor details at expense of more important tasks

CC. Fourteen General Principles of Management
1. Division of work
2. Authority and responsibility
3. Discipline
4. Unity of command
5. Unity of direction
6. Subordination of individual interest to general interest
7. Remuneration of personnel
8. Centralization
9. Scalar chain
10. Order
11. Equity
12. Stability of tenure of personnel
13. Initiative
14. Esprit de corps

DD. Change

Bringing about change is perhaps attempted more often, and yet less well understood, than anything else the supervisor does. How do people generally react to change? (People tend to resist change that is imposed upon them by other individuals or circumstances.

Change is characteristic of every situation. It is a part of every real endeavor where the efforts of people are concerned.

1. Why do people resist change?
   People may resist change because of:
   a. Fear of the unknown
   b. Implied criticism
   c. Unpleasant experiences in the past
   d. Fear of loss of status
   e. Threat to the ego
   f. Fear of loss of economic stability

2. How can we best overcome the resistance to change?
   In initiating change, take these steps:
   a. Get ready to sell
   b. Identify sources of help
   c. Anticipate objections
   d. Sell benefits
   e. Listen in depth
   f. Follow up

II. Brief Topical Summaries

   A. Who/What is the Supervisor?
      1. The supervisor is often called the "highest level employee and the lowest level manager."
      2. A supervisor is a member of both management and the work group. He acts as a bridge between the two.
      3. Most problems in supervision are in the area of human relations, or people problems.
      4. Employees expect: Respect, opportunity to learn and to advance, and a sense of belonging, and so forth.
      5. Supervisors are responsible for directing people and organizing work. Planning is of paramount importance.
      6. A position description is a set of duties and responsibilities inherent to a given position.
      7. It is important to keep the position description up-to-date and to provide each employee with his own copy.

   B. The Sociology of Work
      1. People are alike in many ways; however, each individual is unique.
      2. The supervisor is challenged in getting to know employee differences. Acquiring skills in evaluating individuals is an asset.
      3. Maintaining meaningful working relationships in the organization is of great importance.
      4. The supervisor has an obligation to help individuals to develop to their fullest potential.
      5. Job rotation on a planned basis helps to build versatility and to maintain interest and enthusiasm in work groups.
      6. Cross training (job rotation) provides backup skills.

7. The supervisor can help reduce tension by maintaining a sense of humor, providing guidance to employees, and by making reasonable and timely decisions. Employees respond favorably to working under reasonably predictable circumstances.
8. Change is characteristic of all managerial behavior. The supervisor must adjust to changes in procedures, new methods, technological changes, and to a number of new and sometimes challenging situations.
9. To overcome the natural tendency for people to resist change, the supervisor should become more skillful in initiating change.

C. Principles and Practices of Supervision
1. Employees should be required to answer to only one superior.
2. A supervisor can effectively direct only a limited number of employees, depending upon the complexity, variety, and proximity of the jobs involved.
3. The organizational chart presents the organization in graphic form. It reflects lines of authority and responsibility as well as interrelationships of units within the organization.
4. Distribution of work can be improved through an analysis using the "Work Distribution Chart."
5. The "Work Distribution Chart" reflects the division of work within a unit in understandable form.
6. When related tasks are given to an employee, he has a better chance of increasing his skills through training.
7. The individual who is given the responsibility for tasks must also be given the appropriate authority to insure adequate results.
8. The supervisor should delegate repetitive, routine work. Preparation of recurring reports, maintaining leave and attendance records are some examples.
9. Good discipline is essential to good task performance. Discipline is reflected in the actions of employees on the job in the absence of supervision.
10. Disciplinary action may have to be taken when the positive aspects of discipline have failed. Reprimand, warning, and suspension are examples of disciplinary action.
11. If a situation calls for a reprimand, be sure it is deserved and remember it is to be done in private.

D. Dynamic Leadership
1. A style is a personal method or manner of exerting influence.
2. Authoritarian leaders often see themselves as the source of power and authority.
3. The democratic leader often perceives the group as the source of authority and power.
4. Supervisors tend to do better when using the pattern of leadership that is most natural for them.
5. Social scientists suggest that the effective supervisor use the leadership style that best fits the problem or circumstances involved.
6. All four styles—telling, selling, consulting, joining—have their place. Using one does not preclude using the other at another time.

7. The theory X point of view assumes that the average person dislikes work, will avoid it whenever possible, and must be coerced to achieve organizational objectives.
8. The theory Y point of view assumes that the average person considers work to be a natural as play, and, when the individual is committed, he requires little supervision or direction to accomplish desired objectives.
9. The leader's basic assumptions concerning human behavior and human nature affect his actions, decisions, and other managerial practices.
10. Dissatisfaction among employees is often present, but difficult to isolate. The supervisor should seek to weaken dissatisfaction by keeping promises, being sincere and considerate, keeping employees informed, and so forth.
11. Constructive suggestions should be encouraged during the natural progress of the work.

E. Processes for Solving Problems
1. People find their daily tasks more meaningful and satisfying when they can improve them.
2. The causes of problems, or the key factors, are often hidden in the background. Ability to solve problems often involves the ability to isolate them from their backgrounds. There is some substance to the cliché that some persons "can't see the forest for the trees."
3. New procedures are often developed from old ones. Problems should be broken down into manageable parts. New ideas can be adapted from old one.
4. People think differently in problem-solving situations. Using a logical, patterned approach is often useful. One approach found to be useful includes these steps:
   a. Define the problem
   b. Establish objectives
   c. Get the facts
   d. Weigh and decide
   e. Take action
   f. Evaluate action

F. Training for Results
1. Participants respond best when they feel training is important to them.
2. The supervisor has responsibility for the training and development of those who report to him.
3. When training is delegated to others, great care must be exercised to insure the trainer has knowledge, aptitude, and interest for his work as a trainer.
4. Training (learning) of some type goes on continually. The most successful supervisor makes certain the learning contributes in a productive manner to operational goals.
5. New employees are particularly susceptible to training. Older employees facing new job situations require specific training, as well as having need for development and growth opportunities.
6. Training needs require continuous monitoring.
7. The training officer of an agency is a professional with a responsibility to assist supervisors in solving training problems.

8. Many of the self-development steps important to the supervisor's own growth are equally important to the development of peers and subordinates. Knowledge of these is important when the supervisor consults with others on development and growth opportunities.

G. Health, Safety, and Accident Prevention
1. Management-minded supervisors take appropriate measures to assist employees in maintaining health and in assuring safe practices in the work environment.
2. Effective safety training and practices help to avoid injury and accidents.
3. Safety should be a management goal. All infractions of safety which are observed should be corrected without exception.
4. Employees' safety attitude, training and instruction, provision of safe tools and equipment, supervision, and leadership are considered highly important factors which contribute to safety and which can be influenced directly by supervisors.
5. When accidents do occur, they should be investigated promptly for very important reasons, including the fact that information which is gained can be used to prevent accidents in the future.

H. Equal Employment Opportunity
1. The supervisor should endeavor to treat all employees fairly, without regard to religion, race, sex, or national origin.
2. Groups tend to reflect the attitude of the leader. Prejudice can be detected even in very subtle form. Supervisors must strive to create a feeling of mutual respect and confidence in every employee.
3. Complete utilization of all human resources is a national goal. Equitable consideration should be accorded women in the work force, minority-group members, the physically and mentally handicapped, and the older employee. The important question is: "Who can do the job?"
4. Training opportunities, recognition for performance, overtime assignments, promotional opportunities, and all other personnel actions are to be handled on an equitable basis.

I. Improving Communications
1. Communications is achieving understanding between the sender and the receiver of a message. It also means sharing information—the creation of understanding.
2. Communication is basic to all human activity. Words are means of conveying meanings; however, real meanings are in people.
3. There are very practical differences in the effectiveness of one-way, impersonal, and two-way communications. Words spoken face-to-face are better understood. Telephone conversations are effective, but lack the rapport of person-to-person exchanges. The whole person communicates.
4. Cooperation and communication in an organization go hand in hand. When there is a mutual respect between people, spelling out rules and procedures for communicating is unnecessary.
5. There are several barriers to effective communications. These include failure to listen with respect and understanding, lack of skill in feedback, and misinterpreting the meanings of words used by the speaker. It is also common

practice to listen to what we want to hear, and tune out things we do not want to hear.
6. Communication is management's chief problem. The supervisor should accept the challenge to communicate more effectively and to improve interagency and intra-agency communications.
7. The supervisor may often plan for and conduct meetings. The planning phase is critical and may determine the success or the failure of a meeting.
8. Speaking before groups usually requires extra effort. Stage fright may never disappear completely, but it can be controlled.

J. Self-Development
1. Every employee is responsible for his own self-development.
2. Toastmaster and toastmistress clubs offer opportunities to improve skills in oral communications.
3. Planning for one's own self-development is of vital importance. Supervisors know their own strengths and limitations better than anyone else.
4. Many opportunities are open to aid the supervisor in his developmental efforts, including job assignments; training opportunities, both governmental and non-governmental—to include universities and professional conferences and seminars.
5. Programmed instruction offers a means of studying at one's own rate.
6. Where difficulties may arise from a supervisor's being away from his work for training, he may participate in televised home study or correspondence courses to meet his self-development needs.

K. Teaching and Training
1. The Teaching Process
Teaching is encouraging and guiding the learning activities of students toward established goals. In most cases this process consists of five steps: preparation, presentation, summarization, evaluation, and application.

   a. Preparation
   Preparation is two-fold in nature; that of the supervisor and the employee. Preparation by the supervisor is absolutely essential to success. He must know what, when, where, how, and whom he will teach. Some of the factors that should be considered are:
   1) The objectives
   2) The materials needed
   3) The methods to be used
   4) Employee participation
   5) Employee interest
   6) Training aids
   7) Evaluation
   8) Summarization

   Employee preparation consists in preparing the employee to receive the material. Probably the most important single factor in the preparation of the employee is arousing and maintaining his interest. He must know the objectives of the training, why he is there, how the material can be used, and its importance to him.

b. Presentation
In presentation, have a carefully designed plan and follow it. The plan should be accurate and complete, yet flexible enough to meet situations as they arise. The method of presentation will be determined by the particular situation and objectives.

c. Summary
A summary should be made at the end of every training unit and program. In addition, there may be internal summaries depending on the nature of the material being taught. The important thing is that the trainee must always be able to understand how each part of the new material relates to the whole.

d. Application
The supervisor must arrange work so the employee will be given a chance to apply new knowledge or skills while the material is still clear in his mind and interest is high. The trainee does not really know whether he has learned the material until he has been given a chance to apply it. If the material is not applied, it loses most of its value.

e. Evaluation
The purpose of all training is to promote learning. To determine whether the training has been a success or failure, the supervisor must evaluate this learning.
In the broadest sense, evaluation includes all the devices, methods, skills, and techniques used by the supervisor to keep himself and the employees informed as to their progress toward the objectives they are pursuing. The extent to which the employee has mastered the knowledge, skills, and abilities, or changed his attitudes, as determined by the program objectives, is the extent to which instruction has succeeded or failed.
Evaluation should not be confined to the end of the lesson, day, or program but should be used continuously. We shall note later the way this relates to the rest of the teaching process.

2. Teaching Methods
A teaching method is a pattern of identifiable student and instructor activity used in presenting training material.
All supervisors are faced with the problem of deciding which method should be used at a given time.

a. Lecture
The lecture is direct oral presentation of material by the supervisor. The present trend is to place less emphasis on the trainer's activity and more on that of the trainee.

b. Discussion
Teaching by discussion or conference involves using questions and other techniques to arouse interest and focus attention upon certain areas, and by doing so creating a learning situation. This can be one of the most

valuable methods because it gives the employees an opportunity to express their ideas and pool their knowledge.

    c. Demonstration
The demonstration is used to teach how something works or how to do something. It can be used to show a principle or what the results of a series of actions will be. A well-staged demonstration is particularly effective because it shows proper methods of performance in a realistic manner.

    d. Performance
Performance is one of the most fundamental of all learning techniques or teaching methods. The trainee may be able to tell how a specific operation should be performed but he cannot be sure he knows how to perform the operation until he has done so.
As with all methods, there are certain advantages and disadvantages to each method.

    e. Which Method to Use
Moreover, there are other methods and techniques of teaching. It is difficult to use any method without other methods entering into it. In any learning situation, a combination of methods is usually more effective than any one method alone.

Finally, evaluation must be integrated into the other aspects of the teaching-learning process.

It must be used in the motivation of the trainees; it must be used to assist in developing understanding during the training; and it must be related to employee application of the results of training.

This is distinctly the role of the supervisor.

GLOSSARY OF TRAFFIC CONTROL TERMS

TABLE OF CONTENTS

	Page
Access Road ... Desire Line	1
Divided Street ... Left Turn Lane	2
Manual Traffic Control ... Passenger Vehicle	3
Passenger (Transit) Volume ... Separate Turning Lane	4
Shoulder ... Traffic Accident	5
Traffic Actuated Controller ... Uninterrupted Flow	6
Vehicle ... Zone (Origin-Destination Studies)	7

GLOSSARY OF TRAFFIC CONTROL TERMS

A

ACCESS ROAD - Public roads, existing or proposed, needed to provide essential access to military installation and facilities, or to industrial installations and facilities in the activities of which there is specific defense interest. Roads within the boundaries of military reservation are excluded from this definition unless such roads have been dedicated to public use and are not subject to closure.

ACCIDENT SPOT MAP - An area or installation map showing the location of vehicle accidents by means of symbols. Symbols may represent accidents classified as to daylight hours, night hours, injury or death.

ANGLE PARKING - Parking where the longitudinal axes of vehicles form an angle with the alignment of the roadway.

C

CENTER LINE - A line marking the center of a roadway between traffic moving in opposite direction.

COLLISION DIAGRAM - A plan of an intersection or section of roadway on which reported accidents are diagramed by means of arrows showing manner of collision.

COMBINED CONDITION AND COLLISION DIAGRAM - A condition diagram upon which the reported accidents are diagramed by means of arrows showing manner of collision.

CONDITION DIAGRAM - A plan of an intersection or section of roadway showing all objects and physical conditions having a bearing on traffic movement and safety at that location. Usually these are scaled drawings.

CORDON COUNTS - A count of all vehicles and persons entering and leaving a district (cordon area) during a designated period of time.

CORDON AREA - The district bounded by the cordon line and included in a cordon count.

CROSSWALK - Any portion of a roadway at an intersection or elsewhere distinctly indicated for pedestrian crossing by lines or other markings on the surface. Also, that part of a roadway at an intersection included within the connections of the lateral lines of the sidewalks on opposite sides of the traffic way measured from the curbs, or in the absence of curbs, from the edges of the traversable roadway.

D

DELAY - The time consumed while traffic or a specified component of traffic is impeded in its movement by some element over which it has no control usually expressed in seconds per vehicle.

DESIRE LINE - A straight line between the point of origin and point of destination of a trip without regard to routes of travel (used in connection with an origin-destination study).

DIVIDED STREET - A two-way road on which traffic in one direction of travel is separated from that in the opposite direction by a directional separator. Such a road has two or more roadways.

E

85 PERCENTILE SPEED - That speed below which 85 percent of the traffic unit's travel, and above which 15 percent travel.

F

FIXED-TIME CONTROLLER - An automatic controller for supervising the operation of traffic control signals in accordance with a predetermined fixed time cycle and divisions thereof.

FIXED-TIME TRAFFIC SIGNAL - A traffic signal operated by a fixed-time controller.

FLASHING BEACON - A section of a standard traffic signal head, or a similar type device, having a yellow or red lens in each face, which is illuminated by rapid intermittent flashes.

FLASHING TRAFFIC SIGNAL - A traffic control signal used as a flashing beacon.

FLOATING CAR - An automobile driven in the traffic flow at the average speed of the surrounding vehicles.

FLOW DIAGRAM - The graphical representation of the traffic volumes on a road or street network or section thereof, showing by means of bands the relative volumes using each section of roadway during a given period of time, usually 1 hour.

H

HIGH FREQUENCY ACCIDENT LOCATION - A specific location where a large number of traffic accidents have occurred.

I

INTERSECTION APPROACH - That portion of an intersection leg which is used by traffic approaching the intersection.

L

LATERAL CLEARANCE - The distance between the edge of pavement and any lateral obstruction.

LATERAL OBSTRUCTION - Any fixed object located adjacent to the traveled way which reduces the transverse dimensions of the roadway.

LEFT TURN LANE - A lane within the normal surfaced width reserved for left turning vehicles.

M

MANUAL TRAFFIC CONTROL - The use of-hand signals or manually operated devices by traffic control personnel to control traffic.

MANUAL COUNTER - A tallying device which is operated by hand.

MASS TRANSPORTATION - Movement of large groups of persons.

MULTIAXLE TRUCK - A truck which has more than two axles.

O

OCCUPANCY RATIO -The average number-of occupants per vehicle (including the driver).

ODOMETER -A device on a vehicle for measuring the distance traveled, usually as a cumulative total, but sometimes also for individual trips, with an indicator on the instrument panel where it is usually combined with a speedometer indicator, or in the hub of a wheel in some trucks.

OFF-PEAK PERIOD - That portion of the day in which traffic volumes are relatively light.

OFFSET LANES - Additional lanes used for traffic which is heavier in one direction. Also known as unbalanced lanes.

OFF-STREET PARKING - Lots and garages intended for parking entirely off streets and alleys. street and alleys (may be angle or parallel parking) for parking of vehicles.

ORIGIN DESTINATION STUDIES - A study of the origins and destinations of trips of vehicles and passengers. Usually included in the study are all trips within, or passing through, into or out of a selected area.

OVERALL SPEED - The total distance traversed divided by the travel time. Usually expressed in miles per hour and includes all delays.

OVERALL TIME - The time of travel, including stops and delays except those off the traveled way.

P

PARALLEL PARKING - Parking where the longitudinal axis of vehicles are parallel to alignment of the roadway so that the vehicles are facing in the same direction as the movement of adjacent vehicular traffic.

PARKING DURATION - Length of time a vehicle is parked.

PASSENGER VEHICLE - A free-wheeled, self-propelled vehicle designed for the transportation of persons but limited in seating capacity to not more than seven passengers, not including the driver. It includes taxicabs, limousines, and station wagons, but does not include motorcycles. (In capacity studies, also includes light reconnaissance vehicles, and pickup trucks.)

PASSENGER (TRANSIT) VOLUME - The total number of public transit occupants being transported in a period of time.

PEAK PERIOD - That portion of the day in which maximum traffic volumes are experienced.

PEDESTRIAN - Any person afoot. For purpose of accident classification, this will be interpreted to include any person riding in or upon a device moved or designed for movement by human power or the force of gravity, except bicycles, including stilts, skates, skis, sleds, toy wagons, and scooters.

PERCENT OF GRADE - The slope in the longitudinal direction of the pavement expressed in percent which is the number of units of change in elevation per 100 units of horizontal distance.

PERCENT OF GREEN TIME - The percentage of green time allotted to the direction of travel being studies.

PROPERTY DAMAGE - Damage to property as a result of a motor vehicle accident that may be a basis of a claim for compensation. Does not include compensation for loss of life or for personal injuries.

PUBLIC HIGHWAYS - The entire width between property lines, or boundary lines, of every way or place of which any part is open to use of the public for purposes of vehicular traffic as a matter of right or custom.

PUBLIC TRANSIT - The public passenger carryi ng service afforded by vehicles following regular routes and making specified stops.

R

REFLECTORIZE - The application of some material to traffic control devices or hazards which will return to the eyes of the road user some portion of the light from his vehicle headlights, thereby producing a brightness which attracts attention.

REGULATORY DEVICE - A device used to indicate the required method of traffic movement or use of the public traffic way.

REGULATORY SIGN - A sign used to indicate the required method of traffic movement or use of the traffic way.

RIGHT TURN LANE - A lane within the normal surfaced width reserved for right turning vehicles.

ROADWAY - That portion of a traffic way including shoulders, improved, designed, or ordinarily used for vehicle traffic.

S

SEPARATE TURNING LANE - Added traffic lane which is separated from the intersection area by an island or unpaved area. It may be wide enough for one or two line operation

SHOULDER - The portion of the roadway contiguous with the traveled way for accommodation of stopped vehicles, for emergency use, and for lateral support of base and surface courses.

SIGHT DISTANCES - The length of roadway visible to the driver of a passenger vehicle at any given point on the roadway when the view is unobstructed by traffic.

SIGNAL CYCLE - The total time required for one complete sequence of the intervals of a traffic signal.

SIGNAL CONTROLLER - A complete electrical mechanism for controlling the operation of traffic control signals, including the timer and all necessary auxiliary apparatus mounted in a cabinet.

SIGNAL FACE - That part of a signal head provided for controlling traffic from a single direction.

SIGNAL HEAD - An assembly containing one or more signal faces that may be designated accordingly as one-way, two-way, multi-way.

SIGNAL PHASE - A part of the total time cycle allocated to movements receiving the right-of-way or to any combination ments receiving the right-of-way simultaneously during one

SIMPLE INTERSECTION - An intersection of two traffic ways, approaches.

SPEED - The rate of movement of a vehicle, generally expressed in miles per hour.

STOPPING SIGHT DISTANCE –The distance required by a drive of a vehicle, given speed, to bring vehicle to a stop after and object becomes visible.

STREET WIDTH - The width of the paved or traveled portion of the roadway.

T

THROUGH MOVEMENT - (See THROUGH TRAFFIC)

THROUGH STREET - A street on which traffic is given the right-of-way so that vehicles entering or crossing the street must yield the right-of-way.

THROUGH TRAFFIC - Traffic proceeding through a military installation or portion not originating in or destined to that military installation or portion thereof.

TIME CYCLE - (See SIGNAL CYCLE)

TRAFFIC - Pedestrians, ridden or herded animals, vehicles, street cars, and other conveyances, either singly or together, while using any street for purposes of travel.

TRAFFIC ACCIDENT - Any accident involving a motor vehicle in motion that results in death, injury, or property damage.

TRAFFIC ACTUATED CONTROLLER- An automatic controller for supervising the operation of traffic control signals in accordance with the immediate and varying demands of traffic as registered with the-controller by means of detectors.

TRAFFIC CONTROL - All measures except those of a structural kind that serve to control and guide traffic and to promote road safety.

TRAFFIC CONTROL DEVICE - A Traffic control device is any sign, signal, marking, or device placed or erected for the purpose of regulating, warning, or guiding traffic.

TRAFFIC DEMAND - The volume of traffic desiring to use a particular route or facility.

TRAFFIC ENGINEERING - That phase of engineering that deals with the planning and geometric design of streets, highways, and abutting lands, and with traffic operations thereon, as their use is related to the safe, convenient, and economic transportation of persons and goods.

TRAFFIC FLOW - The movement of vehicles on a roadway.

TRAFFIC FLOW PATTERN - The distribution of traffic volumes on a street or highway network~

TRAFFIC GENERATOR - A traffic producing area such as a post exchange, parking lot, or administrative center.

TRAFFIC SIGNAL INTERVAL - Anyone of the several divisions of the total time cycle during which signal indications do not change.

TRAFFICWAY - The entire width between property lines (or other boundary lines) of every way or place of which any part is open to use of public for purposes of vehicular traffic as a matter of right or custom.

TRANSIT VEHICLE - A passenger carrying vehicle, such as a bus or streetcar which follows regular routes and makes specific stops.

TRAVEL TIME- The total elapsed time from the origin to destination of a trip.

TURNING MOVEMENT - The traffic making a designated turn at an intersection.

TWO-WAY STREETS - A street on which traffic may move in opposite directions simultaneously. It may be either divided or undivided.

TYPE OF ACCIDENT - The kind of motor vehicle accident, such as head-on, right-angle, etc.

TYPE OF SURFACE - The class of surface such as concrete, asphalt, gravel, etc.

U

UNINTERRRUPTED FLOW - The flow of-vehicles under ideal conditions resulting in unrestricted movement.

V

VEHICLE - Every device in, upon, or by which any person or property is or may be transported or drawn upon a highway, except those devices moved by human power or used exclusively upon stationary rails or tracks.

VEHICULE OCCUPANCY - The average number of occupants per automobile, including the driver.

VOLUME - The number of vehicles passing a given point during a specified period of time.

W

WARNING SIGN - A sign used to indicate conditions that are actually or potentially hazardous to highway users.

WARRANT - Formally stated conditions that have been accepted as minimum requirements for justifying installation of a traffic control device or regulation.

Z

ZONE (ORIGIN-DESTINATION STUDIES) -- A division of an area established for the purpose of analyzing origin-destination studies. It may be bounded by physical barriers such as rivers and highways, or may be the location of individual work organizations that have duty stations in relatively close proximity.

184

www.ingramcontent.com/pod-product-compliance
Lightning Source LLC
Chambersburg PA
CBHW080732230426
43665CB00020B/2710